The
PATH
OF

HEAL
ING

The PATH OF HEALING

H. K. Challoner

A QUEST BOOK

THE THEOSOPHICAL PUBLISHING HOUSE

Wheaton, Ill., U.S.A.
Madras, India / London, England

Originally published by the Theosophical
Publishing House, London.

Second Quest edition published by the
Theosophical Publishing House, Wheaton,
Illinois, a department of The Theosophical
Society in America, 1982.

Library of Congress Cataloging in Publication Data

Mills, Janet Melanie Ailsa, 1894—
    The path of healing.

    (A Quest book)
    1. Theosophy. 2. Mental healing. I. Title.
[DNLM: 1. Mental healing. WB880 C437p 1972a]
BP573.H4M5   1976   615'.852   76-3660
ISBN 0-8356-0480-2

Printed in The United States of America

To
"The Patient"
with affection

INTRODUCTION TO THE
SECOND EDITION

THE interest shown in many new and unorthodox methods of healing has been increasing in recent years. More and more practitioners are to be found claiming to be able to treat successfully many forms of illness which have hitherto baffled the orthodox.

There seems little doubt that some of these claims have been justified, so much so that a few cures have even been hailed as miraculous.

We will only consider here a few forms of healing by those who possess rare kinds of sensitivity such as extra-sensory perception which enables them to see or sense symptoms which have escaped orthodox methods; magnetic healers and those who believe that they are controlled by unseen agencies or by the spirits of the dead.

This latter form of treatment is rightly classed as "psychic" and is usually transmitted through a medium either in trance or under direction while remaining conscious.

Whether such treatments are efficacious or not must clearly depend largely upon the vision, knowledge and indeed often the wisdom of the practitioner just as ordinary medical treatment does, but in this case it depends also upon the degree of sensitivity and the integrity of the medium.

But it must always be taken into account that however devoted, selfless and eager to help sufferers the controlling entity may be, unless he has passed into the afterlife with some ordinary medical knowledge and training he can be just as capable of making serious mistakes in diagnosis and methods of treatment as an inefficient doctor on earth.

For it does not follow that because you are "dead", that is to say have merely moved into another dimension, you automatically acquire knowledge and ability you did not possess while in a physical body. This patent fact is often overlooked.

Unfortunately many mediums in their eagerness to help, offer themselves to any entity who claims to be a "healer". But unless such a medium possesses reliable clairvoyant vision and has been trained in psychology and even has some knowledge of philosophy, that is to say is mentally well equipped to pass judgment, she—or he—has clearly no means of checking the nature of the entity who may respond to the invitation. It is not safe to have confidence that all "guides" who announce that they come from a "very high plane" actually do so. To many, even, whose intentions are of the best, the plane upon which they find themselves may indeed seem high relative to the density of the material world they have left, just as it does to the medium. But this does not mean that it is much above the lower astral plane which is only the next stage up—so to speak—from the physical. Consequently deceptions may arise which could put the patient in jeopardy.

Of course there are many cases of psychic healing in which the patient may be cured, so far as physical symptoms are concerned; but, as will later be shown, there are factors at far deeper levels involved in any cure which is to be genuine and lasting.

Magnetic treatment is of a different nature, although it can also be transmitted through a medium and many forms of psychic healing might also be classed as magnetic.

Very often the healer is himself powerfully charged with some specific form of energy which he can transfer to the patient. The effect of this stimulation by what might be termed the "life-force" or "prana" is in some cases quite dramatic. But here again the real efficacy of such a recharging of the cell-life depends upon the healer's own understanding and control of the forces he is manipulating plus his ability to sense the patient's real needs and regulate and direct the flow accordingly. Unless he is capable of this such methods of treatment can also be dangerous. For it is obvious that to inject a powerful stream of energy (which can be destructive as well as creative according to the specific rate of the charge used) into, say, an ulcer or a growth could stimulate into activity the very condition which the healer sets out to dissipate. There is also the psychological effect to be considered. Most sick people are in a low, negative and apprehensive state when they go to a healer. An overdose of energy could for the moment make them feel cured and cause them to be unduly elated. But unless the force had been wisely distributed, the resulting reaction of disappointment would be all the more severe and the general condition suffer in consequence.

Etheric healing methods are based on the fact that the body has counterparts in matter so subtle that no ordinary instruments can register their presence. Clairvoyants can often see these etheric and astral bodies as they are called. It is now claimed that the existence of the etheric has been scientifically proved by means of the Kilner screens which actually made it visible.

The etheric acts as a transmitting and distributing agent for the life-force. Consequently if disturbances take place within it so that certain currents of force do not reach their physical counterparts as they should, the physical body is deprived of its vital needs and illness or nervous exhaustion results.

In this case the clairvoyant healer would attempt to correct those lines of force which have become diverted or short-circuited and redirect them to the centres of the body which were not being properly "fed". This is sometimes done by means of a kind of etheric massage which is performed just above the afflicted parts and is a method of tackling the trouble behind the scenes, from an anterior and not as yet generally recognized source of possible disturbance.

Yet, even this, although certainly attempting to deal with illness at a rather deeper level than normal, is still working on effects rather than upon basic causes and also depends on the capacity of the healer to judge what the real need of the patient is and above all just what and how much should be given him.

In fact all these methods, including those of orthodox medicine which is still probably the most reliable of them all are, from a much more radical inner point of view, attempting in the main to remove or alleviate *symptoms* and are seldom able to treat the originating causes of which virtually all disorders in the economy of mankind are the outcome.

Deep analysis sometimes claims to have uncovered these causes when its practitioners succeed in probing as far back, even, as before actual birth. But is even this far enough? Have they reached the *cause of the cause*?

There is one other important method to be noted. This is healing by means of invocation or prayer: the attempt to reach above the levels upon which the majority of other forms of healing operate. Here the practitioner is calling upon spiritual wisdom, power and insight, attempting to penetrate into that realm where the *real* needs of the sick person are known and from which the appropriate force to deal with these needs in the right way must surely come.

While there have been many remarkable instances of response to prayer, it is still impossible to say to what an extent this only temporarily removes symptoms rather than the deeper causes of the condition. And by "temporarily" we mean, in every case, for this life only. This is the crux of the whole matter.

But one thing is certain about the efficacy of prayer, the energy which comes from these higher levels will be regulated solely by the patient's *real* needs at the moment. Thus he cannot fail to be the recipient of spiritual energy which will uplift and strengthen him to the extent, of course, that he is capable of response, and that response can come even if consciously he is unaware of what is being done for him. In any case there are no dangers here.

I have spoken above of the "cause of the cause". Where are the real roots of our condition to be found? Unfortunately we seem seldom if ever to come into this world "trailing clouds of glory". Quite the contrary. The majority of us are born with an almost certain prospect of sickness, imbalance and disturbances, physical, emotional or mental, the seeds of which seem to have already implanted in us even before birth.

Unless one believes in pure chance, or that each individual is a newly created "soul", certain questions must arise. Why do we each bring with us not only certain qualities, tendencies and characteristics, but also what might be called our "fate", that which determines why we have been born in a specific family and environment at a specific time? What is the true originating cause of each of us being *ourself* and all that that implies? To answer "genes" is clearly no answer because it does not tell us why we have inherited these genes, which anyhow do not provide us with all the answers and can only cover a very limited number of factors.

But there are other answers which the average doctor and also a great many psychic healers do not recognize as determining factors.

These can be classed generically under what in the East is called Karma; that is to say the great universal spiritual law of Cause and Effect.

It is knowledge of this which alone can readily determine

not only the method of cure which could be effective but also whether any cure is possible in this life. In other words whether the patient is *ready* to be cured. Needless to say only those with more than human vision could know this. It may be significant that even Jesus, full of love and compassion as he was, seems only to have cured a chosen few.

May not the words: "Thy sins be forgiven thee" give us a clue? Would anyone be capable of obeying the injunction: "Go and sin no more" if he had not already nearly reached the end of the road to perfection but had perhaps not yet been able to succeed in expressing it in his personality and needed only an extraordinary stimulus to enable him to do so?

This form of healing would, of course, be what might be called basic healing, the elimination of the true *cause* of the cause, that is to say "inhibited soul life"—a very revealing phrase used by a great spiritual expert in the healing art.

But clearly very few people have reached the stage when such basic healing is possible.

At this point the reader may reasonably object: "This is ridiculous! Millions of people are healed even of such terrible diseases as cancer."

Of course they are and must be if the human race—and especially the individual—is to learn all the lessons man comes on earth to learn, one of which is to discover how to cure himself finally of every tendency to disease.

Who is ready and who is not ready for any specific sickness of body, emotion or mind to be cured cannot be known. Meanwhile all the time medical and some degree of psychological knowledge increases, and when spiritual knowledge is added to this then indeed true and permanent cures will be possible so clearing the way for future lives no longer so tormented and frustrated by all the ills to which the personality is heir.

The treatment of which this book is a record was given by one who knew far more of the causes behind illness than the average healer and describes the attempt to show his patient the way by means of which a permanent and lasting cure could be achieved.

This particular patient had been ill since childhood. Born into a family with a bad medical history she inherited tendencies to various forms of physical weakness and glandular imbalance which affected her whole nervous system. These difficulties were increased by her upbringing and the attitudes of those about her. The conflicting elements in family relationships caused emotional stress, her longing for affection being thwarted at every turn. This increased her natural ambition and desire for recognition and success. As she grew up these emotional conflicts aroused resentment and bitterness, but above all a condition of insecurity and fear.

Her family were atheists and she had very little ethical training, the general attitude being: "Get all you can out of life regardless of other considerations."

But there were compensating factors. Chief of these were well-developed mental faculties, insight into her own character and the ability to learn from mistakes. From her early years she had a yearning for something more satisfying than the social round which engaged her elders. She had also an inner conviction that there must exist answers not only to all the questions regarding the meaning and purpose of life which exercised her mind but also a reason for her increasing sickness and what she felt to be the injustice of the fate which denied her everything she really desired; love first of all, but also greater opportunities for the expression of a powerful creative urge which nothing trivial would satisfy.

None of the theories in the books she devoured really gave her a feeling of conviction except that of reincarnation which she instinctively accepted but was incapable

of understanding in depth or applying to her own destiny.
As years went by she spent more and more time consulting every type of specialist both in England and abroad
in search of a cure and when all these failed turned to
unorthodox methods and to psychics in the hope, always
vain, of some kind of help or even some reassurance of
happiness to come.

At last in despair she made a desperate appeal to an
unspecified source she vaguely identified with some higher
beneficent Power, not only for relief from pain but to be
shown why she had always been so afflicted and, if it
was not already too late to hope for a cure, to be helped to
adjust herself better to accepting her condition so that
she could bear her increasing pain. But, above all to be
shown how to control the dark pressure of her morbid
fears.

Eventually she was drawn, apparently by chance, to the
present writer who had already had the experience of
being overshadowed and used for writing and painting.

I have used the term "overshadowed" advisedly, as at
no time had there been any question of trance and I had
always been allowed complete freedom to stop the work at
any moment I chose.

A brief word as to the method employed will be useful
here although the whole process and the way it began is
described in detail in two earlier books produced under
the same influence.*

I had never possessed any psychic powers nor had I been
interested in psychic phenomena—quite the contrary.
But when originally the sudden "overshadowing" took
place the ability to write automatically developed almost
from one day to the next. At first the hand was guided,
but very soon hand and mind were co-ordinated. Words
and ideas were projected so powerfully into my mind,

* *The Wheel of Rebirth* and *Regents of the Seven Spheres*, published by
Theosophical Publishing House London Ltd.

presumably by some form of telepathic transference, that it was as easy to speak them aloud as to write them down. The same type of control was used for drawing and painting, although in this case the shapes and colours were precipitated into the mind before the hand was moved to reproduce them.

So when I was impressed to help this patient it was not difficult for the hands to be guided to any place on the body when it was necessary to give a form of what I have described as etheric massage. When the talks started this often preceded them in order to help the patient to relax and attain an attitude of quiet receptivity and gain confidence. But I must emphasize that no type of hypnosis was ever used.

I had been giving the patient some ordinary massage in order to try and relieve an acute attack of pain when quite suddenly I became aware of the well-known vibration which I had not felt for some time.

The entity whom I shall call the Teacher spoke only for a few moments. He told her that he had come in response to her cry, not only for healing, but to be given greater understanding of the causes for her life-long suffering which not all her searching and reading had been able to explain. There were special reasons why this help could be given which, if she decided to put herself in his hands, he would explain later.

While he was prepared to do all that was possible—and permitted—to help her, it was essential that she should agree to try to follow his instructions fully and play her part in a process which might eventually bring her to a point where a greater measure of health and happiness than she had ever known became possible. She must also be prepared to accept, provisionally, many largely unfamiliar ideas not only about herself, but about the world of which she was a part, and to make a genuine effort to put these ideas into effect. He asked her to search her heart and see if she could genuinely accept these conditions, hard though they might be, for he could promise her no easy road. She must be prepared to face many disappointments, setbacks and also some very unpleasant truths about herself.

When he became aware that her attitude was the right and only possible one in order to make such a drastic treatment possible he would return.

Her reaction was, of course, one of immense emotional expectancy. Although at every fresh experiment she had always been buoyed up with hope, each had ended in disappointment. But now at last, it seemed, she might be, if not cured, at least relieved of much of her pain and fear.

Life would be changed, doors would open. Anyone who has been frustrated by illness, whose ambitions have been thwarted, whose life has been a struggle against fate, and who has never known real happiness would understand her mood. She was, moreover, creative by nature, and longed for greater power of self-expression; this would now surely find release. She would do anything, however hard and difficult, that could make this possible. There were, of course, moments of inevitable reaction. She had had so many treatments by what had been called "very high Guides", infallible beings from the next world who had promised her all her desires; they had failed leaving her more disillusioned and sceptical and often worse in health than before.

So she waited in an agony of hope mingled with doubt.

It is at this point that the record of these treatments begins.

About the nature of the Teacher I will not be more specific. At the time I was convinced—as I still am—that behind this work was a definite personality; but as I am not clairvoyant I could not see who was present. However, as I have said, I always became aware of his approach by a very definite vibration, a change in the atmosphere, and also by what I can only call a response throughout my whole being. These states, which I presume are fairly common, are quite impossible to describe to anyone who has not experienced them although they were as real to me as touching a live wire.

There could, I suppose, be other explanations, including the inevitable ones of illusion and auto-suggestion given by the materialist or the sceptic. But such rationalizations, I think, could be ignored in the circumstances in view of the treatments themselves.

As to method, I presume the transmission could have been made through my own superconscious. But what do we yet really know of these states above consciousness? The individual superconscious is often incidentally identified with the Soul. I will not enlarge on this as the Teacher has much to say about the higher state in man.

We are also told that there exist groups of discarnate individuals who are making a special effort at this time of change and confusion in man's thinking to put through to the world new aspects of what has been called the Ancient or Perennial Wisdom. In such a case I presume one of these could take over, so to speak, anyone with the requisite sensitivity who was willing to co-operate and was on the same wavelength or with whom there was a special link from the past. The whole field of such communications between the planes is one of extreme subtlety and dependent upon many different circumstances and variations and very little as yet is known about its techniques. Clearly, whatever the method employed in order to put through the true spiritual teaching, it must be the higher levels of the medium's consciousness which are used because it is only through these that a vibration pure enough for spiritual healing of the nature described could be transmitted to the personality.

It seems to me now, in view of my studies in the thirty or so years since this book was first published, that the actual source whence such help and inspiration emanates is not of major importance. What is important is whether it has that ring of truth which is unmistakable and is empowered, as I feel this to have been, by an unmistakable vibration of love and spiritual illumination; and finally that the teaching given is in complete accord with that of the Great Ones all down the ages.

I must leave it to the readers of this book to make their own judgments upon this.

To return to the treatments themselves.

They are recorded here very largely verbatim. Fortunately the patient possessed a remarkable memory which was aided by her intense concentration at the time they were given. I was also able to recall enough to enable us to write them down immediately the treatments ended. For, as the Teacher said in his last talk, the expenditure of energy that such an effort at communication entailed could hardly have been permissible for the good of one individual alone but must be passed on to a wider public.

Since this particular series was published other talks have been given and I have also received from what I believe to be the same source amplifications of some of the original ideas. These I have included in this edition, weaving them in where they are most appropriate. And for this I am convinced I have received full permission.

When the question arose of reissuing the book I was impressed to make certain small alterations to the actual language which was addressed, it must be remembered, to one specific person; and, as the Teacher said when the treatments began, was addressed to her in the manner best suited to her temperament. Certain phrases have, therefore, been modified in places although where possible the poetic imagery has been retained as this may still appeal to many readers.

So may a number of invocations, exhortations and

prayers which were often given at the end of a treatment; but as in a sense they here tend to break the continuity I have placed them together at the end of the book.

Inevitably throughout the reader will find a certain amount of repetition, not only of words and phrases but also of aspects of the teaching itself, of ideas and training methods.

This was intentional. Whereas the basic principles underlying the whole series of talks were few, in view of their universality they are applicable in one aspect or another to virtually every situation in the life of the average human being.

But as many ideas were new to the patient and at first difficult for her to grasp and to apply, it was essential to explain them in various contexts and prove their relevance to the solution of all kinds of problems and situations.

Another reason for this repetition was the attempt to impress the principles so strongly upon her that in the future she would find herself almost automatically returning to them in order to discover their relevance to whatever problem or situation she found herself facing.

During the treatments, of course, the Teacher was in a position to ascertain the patient's state of mind and to observe from day to day what real progress in understanding had been achieved. He could see what resistances continued to operate even at subconscious levels and what aspects of truth were rejected deliberately because they did not fit in with her preconceptions or desires.

He also knew when some vital point had been grasped, not merely intellectually but at deeper levels, so that it had become a permanent part of her equipment, a weapon she could use in any future conflict between, say, the mind and the emotions.

In the first case he would repeat the more difficult concepts many times, clothing them perhaps in a new guise or expressing them by means of different symbols or allegories, thus adapting them to meet her special requirements.

Many of the talks were naturally concerned to elucidate the patient's particular problems. Some of these are included here as I feel readers may find in them help in their own difficulties. For despite the fact that no two people can have absolutely identical problems, the words addressed to one individual in distress can often strike a note to which another member in the great human family may respond.

In the final count each must seek in any form of teaching for the message which speaks to his own condition and must search his heart for the causes which have brought about his individual problems. He must also learn to perceive his need—that is to say the nature of his "cure"—through an increasing understanding of universal Truth.

If this record should help a single individual to do so, the sufferings which brought about this cry for spiritual enlightenment will have served a deeper than a purely individual purpose.

In conclusion I would like to emphasize that had it not been for the courage, and even more the attitude of receptivity and of faith shown by the patient herself, the power requisite for these treatments would surely not have been forthcoming.

I want, therefore, to thank her in the name of any who may benefit, for her generosity in allowing so much of a private nature to be published and also for her co-operation and invaluable assistance throughout the writing of this book.

H. K. CHALLONER

THE PATH OF HEALING

I

IF you had not been ready to make an attempt to comply with my conditions I would not have the right, nor indeed the power, to offer to help you.

This I know you will understand. It would be useless to deal with the results caused by a poison if it were constantly being absorbed afresh. That is just what has been taking place within the economy of your body and mind for far longer than you can be aware of. Clearly, then, before any process of basic healing can even begin the nature of these subtle poisons and their source must be recognized and their effects understood.

But let there be no misconceptions at the very start. If you expect me to heal you by giving you some magic formula, some elixir of life which will transform you without any serious effort on your part at total collaboration you are expecting the impossible. No such elixir exists. Nor could any exterior power be invoked which could or would alter conditions at all levels that are the result of a long process of development involving many lives and events.

True, apparent miracles of healing do happen. Sudden revelations or insights into Reality can occur which change a man's whole attitude and life-pattern. But what is seldom realized is that when this takes place it is the culmination of deep and unrecognized processes which from within have long been preparing the sufferer for such a genuine and radical form of healing. In other words he has worked through or transmuted the causes which originally brought about the ills from which he has suffered in this life. Keep this in mind.

Without any doubt I can show you the way to ultimate release from your sickness but it is you of your own free will who must set your feet upon that path—no man can walk it but the traveller himself. I can and will suggest remedies, but you cannot be cured if you do not avail yourself of them. I can point out the causes which have been largely instrumental in bringing you to your present condition; but unless you are prepared to make the effort to correct many errors in thinking and living the results you hope for cannot eventuate.

I emphasize this because I do not want you to cherish misconceptions which may lead to bitter disappointment and a return of the old hopeless despair. In any case do not expect results too soon and become disheartened.

I know that to many like yourself who are fully aware that they can never achieve their desires in this life because they are actually unattainable; who are convinced that they are destined to failure and sorrow and have come to see existence itself as compounded of miseries, cruelties, pain and frustration, such efforts as I demand may seem impossible to make at first and any hope I may hold out for a better future but a vain illusion.

I agree that many of your present desires are unattainable and that life can appear meaningless and hopeless *when viewed from the particular angle you have adopted* which up to the present has been the wrong angle. But I do declare to you that most surely there *does exist within yourself* a Power which can change, not the pressures and events of the external world upon your body and mind, but your whole orientation and reaction to these pressures, hence the nature of their impact and influence upon you.

It is to a recognition of and union with this Power that I hope to guide you. For I can assure you that once you have learned how to align yourself with it and be directed by it in all your activities your whole outlook on life will change and this cannot but have an influence upon your health.

But I repeat: this change cannot come about quickly; so do not expect anything of the kind. All real growth is. slow; only by stabilizing itself stage by stage can anything become strong and enduring.

What I can and will give you until you can tap the sources of true healing for yourself are all possible aids towards the attainment of a greater degree of health and peace. But you must realize that they can at best be no more than temporary measures to enable you to continue living and learning until the genuine and lasting curative factors can be brought into effect.

Before I speak to you further about the nature of this Power, this regenerating principle within yourself upon which you can learn to draw, it is essential that you be prepared to accept the possibility that such a centre does exist; this should not be too difficult in view of all your studies, although you have never really grasped basic principles nor been able to relate them to your condition.

I do not ask more than an open-minded attitude at present. Certainly not blind faith. This is a frail candle, too easily extinguished in the fierce winds of modern thought, as you have already discovered. While necessary at a certain stage of man's development to help him on his way, there comes a time when it must be replaced by the torch of understanding which alone can illuminate the path of the wayfarer by the light of proofs so convincing that the attacks of the purely discursive intellect by which you have been so much assailed can no longer have the power to demolish them. It is this torch I hope eventually to put into your hands to guide you upon your way.

Yet at first in order to enable me to do this it is

essential that you attempt to take up an attitude of mind which at least approximates to faith, a readiness to accept what I have to say, if only provisionally.

After all, most people are forced by circumstances to put their faith in the pronouncements of those whose studies have revealed many of the secrets of the natural world and so proved how deceptive man's senses can be. So it is not unreasonable to suggest that you should accept what I have to tell you about wider spheres of knowledge as tenable hypotheses, if no more, until you are in a position to prove or disprove them for yourself. For all I say is based upon the evidence of those experts in the realms of what might be called spiritual science— men who, since remote periods of time, have devoted their lives to the search for Reality.

They all postulate the existence of certain basic laws governing not only the life of the universe but that of the individual, the "microcosm of the macrocosm". They have also revealed through their experiments the manner in which each individual could learn so to order his life in harmony with these laws that the conflicts which cause nearly all his sufferings would cease and he would attain not only to physical health but to peace and happiness.

You will see, therefore, that the way I shall advise you to explore is no new way, although it may sound revolutionary in some of its aspects to the sceptic which you have become. But always remember that it is a path by means of which these great teachers have attained to such superhuman heights of understanding that they have been liberated from those compulsions and the inner as well as outer stresses which cause so much suffering to ordinary men.

This is indeed a tried and tested path, as surely authenticated by the actual experience of both the humble and the great as the path of the earth round the sun has been authenticated by the researches of the astronomers. There need be no doubt, then, either of its validity or its efficacy.

But I would stress again that it remains essentially a path of personal experiment and experience. Only to the extent that the traveller can prove its value for himself can he become expert in his turn.

Man's goal has always been wholeness of being, whether he has recognized it or not; for in all religions that goal is taught to be the will of our Creator. And wholeness among many other qualities and powers includes perfect health. But until body, emotions, mind and soul—that is to say desire, intellect and wisdom—dwell together in harmony this ultimate goal for humanity cannot be attained.

So if you are now genuinely prepared to attempt this journey into wholeness by undergoing the training I can indicate to you, it may be possible that I working from my side and you from yours we may together be able to build for you the foundations of what can become so strong a tower of defence that you will at last be capable of facing fearlessly any storms and tests that life may hold in the future. For you will be drawing upon all those powerful sources of strength and healing within yourself, the existence of which you have as yet hardly begun to recognize.

II

In my last talk I spoke of the existence of certain universal laws and it is these which form the structure upon which the method of healing I shall use is based. So it is essential that you understand something about them before any progress can be made.

But before I speak of them further I must point out that you should not imagine that these can express more than a fraction of the truths of which they are but partial glimpses. By their very nature all forms of words are restrictive, particularly where spiritual concepts are concerned. They crystallize ideas by enclosing them within the shell of concrete images. Thus they often veil rather than reveal their inner content and significance and so can all too easily substitute distorted half-truths and dogmas in the mind of the learner. This is a danger to which you must always be alert and on your guard.

So I would urge you to try and seek for the deeper, more universal meaning behind all I may say and not attach yourself too rigidly to the actual language in which I am forced to clothe my thoughts. For no two people put precisely the same interpretation upon the terms they use.

A listener should always try to identify himself as closely as possible with the speaker's mind, try to find out what he is attempting to express rather than instantly putting his own interpretations upon the words and either agreeing or dissenting without examining their meaning more deeply.

This may not be easy for you at first because you have a quick and critical mind; but at some time in one's development it is essential to make this effort at detachment and begin to consider any new ideas objectively and without prejudice. For how is it possible to judge their merits or demerits until they have been considered from every point of view?

But I will try to adapt the language I use to the particular symbolism and shades of meaning with which you tend to colour your thoughts and will use terms which most clearly express the inner significance of the concepts I am hoping to make clear to you.

The first essential is for you to grasp something of the total pattern of existence.

Begin by trying to imagine the myriads of life-forms, from the most subtle to the most dense, from the smallest particle yet discovered to the inconceivably great island universes, not as separated units or lives but rather as aspects, reflections or facets of one absolute *unity,* a single LIFE manifesting through all that *is.* The names given to this Source of Infinite Potentiality are, as you know, many; some think of It as Creative Mind, others the Divine Will. In this present age many, seeking to define what is indefinable, equate It with energy. But let us use the term God, for this covers every definition, though in the East they wisely give It no name at all, using the word "THAT" or a trinity of names expressing Its qualities since they feel that as It must surpass all mortal modes of expression or imagination It should remain nameless.

But in any case names matter less than most people think. It is the spiritual significance attributed to this incomprehensible Unity of Being, this Wholeness, which is important.

If, then, all that is manifest at whatsoever level arises from a single Source, is a partial reflection of or emanation from some aspect of a WHOLE, it follows that each individual part must be related in the fullest meaning of that word to every other and that nothing in creation can be outside or truly separate from that which *in itself* is single and complete. This means that from greatest to smallest, from the most dense to the most subtle all are imbued with the ONE LIFE, *are* that One Life in manifestation, so must in essence fit together in the divine scheme of things like the separate pieces of a jigsaw puzzle, each in its *reality* contributing to the total significance of the whole, each with its destined part to play in the great emergent pattern of God's will to manifest.

It is only due to the limitations imposed upon any being, however vast his consciousness, by the fact that he *feels* himself to be separate which make him incapable of solving the mystery inherent in the concept of ONENESS or WHOLENESS. For only by becoming consciously identified with the WHOLE could it be known.

But the greater the extent to which consciousness can be expanded the greater the sweep of life it can include; to its extent only then, can it be capable of obtaining a deeper understanding of what this cosmic scheme really represents and what its purpose and goal is.

Certain of the very greatest sages and teachers have attained to insights, fleeting and partial glimpses of some shadows of Reality and it is from their stumbling efforts to express what they well knew to be inexpressible that other seekers have gained intimations of mysteries still infinitely beyond their reach.

It will become clearer to you as you study the pronouncements of such men of vision that in order to begin to understand the deeper meaning of your own life-pattern, your place in your own small part of the scheme of things, it is always essential to keep in mind that you are not the isolated unit you so often seem to yourself to be. On the contrary; you belong to this totality, are one with it. And your relationships, not only with those about you and even with the rest of your world as well as with nature in all her changing forms and aspects, are close and indissoluble. What is more, because of this, you personally have a special and indeed a unique significance. Such a realization is essential to the ultimate attainment of true health and well-being.

Naturally those who tend to concentrate entirely on their own affairs, who centre everything upon themselves and are separative by nature find it particularly difficult to achieve this outlook. And as identification with the personality, its desires and aims, has been very much your own attitude hitherto, it is of vital importance that you make a special effort to attain to this wider vision and to grasp not only intellectually but imaginatively this concept of *wholeness*, the existence of an absolute unity of being which through invisible threads binds not only you but humanity and earth itself, indeed the entire universe, into one organism, one "body of Life".

In order to do so I suggest that you take an imaginative leap whenever you have a period of quiet.

Try to visualize the whole vast cosmos as one pulsating, dynamic, creative field of consciousness which in its densest form manifests as no more than a response to stimuli and at its most subtle is, in some way impossible yet to grasp, *total*, embracing the whole and active throughout wherein all must be known by all in some process of timeless participation. Remember my warning about the use of words. This is only a poor attempt to create a speculative image of truth.

Next try to see the entire universe constructed upon groups of lives, perhaps rather like the cells in a honeycomb, all obeying similar basic laws and all animated by the power of a single Energizing Principle which we might think of as the will of God.

It is by the practice of some exercise such as this and by seeking to discover the correspondences between these lives, from the infinitely great to the infinitely small, and the way in which similar patterns, similar rhythms actually repeat themselves throughout the

Cosmos, that a deeper perception of the meaning of transcendental unity can begin to dawn. Its value is, in reality, to stimulate the faculty of intuition, which is far higher than intellect.

There is a very ancient axiom which may help you, for it expresses the universality of the basic unity of life with great clarity and precision:

> As it is in the Great, so it is in the small;
> As it is Above so it is below;
> As is the Within so is the without;
> There is but one Life and one Law.

And continues by emphasizing the essential unity of ALL.

> There is neither great nor small,
> There is neither above nor below,
> There is neither within nor without
> In the divine Economy.

Mediation upon this will open your eyes to many truths.

By making a practice of trying to discover the correspondences between the pairs of opposites, the above and the below, the within and the without, great and small, light and darkness, good and evil in the world in which you live you will begin to realize how analogous patterns, analogous rhythms and movements repeat themselves not only throughout the universe and in your own world but also in your own life.

For instance by considering the manner in which the inconceivably vast systems revolve round a central nucleus of power you will realize that this pattern is repeated in your own structure which is also powered by a nucleus of energy analogous to the sun of a solar system, your sun being that divine spark of Life which, metaphorically, is said to reside in the heart. Moreover you too are composed of myriads of smaller systems each with its

own nucleus of energy, the formatory forces or little
lives of the body.

The whole universe envisaged thus appears as an
incredibly intricate web of relationships, manifestations of
the One Life. These are ever engaged in cycles of creativity and dissolution by means of which they build themselves up into a totality reflecting the will of their
Progenitor to make manifest what, in an Indian scripture,
is said to be but *one aspect* of the infinite potentiality of the
divine nature. Here Shri Krishna speaking as God says:
"Having pervaded this whole vast cosmos with *one
fragment* of Myself, *I remain.*"

This scheme of system after system in constant flux,
forever being born and forever passing into other expressions of life, applies not only to the realms of dense
matter but also to those of matter in every degree of
subtlety; for matter, however rarefied it may be, is the
universal medium of manifestation, all is divine *substance.*

So far as you are concerned at present, it suffices for
you to try and apply these concepts to the realms of the
body, the emotions, the mind and the spirit. Man possesses actual bodies at all these levels although the last
three are not yet recognized as such by the scientists,
despite the fact that they play a role of major importance so far as health and general well-being are
concerned.

Give much time to the consideration of this brief outline I have sketched for you. Try to grasp the conception
of Life—the divine *Stuff* of being, manifesting on all
these planes and levels in conformity with the basic
rhythm of universal laws.

Imagine every form, dense or subtle coming into
existence by the pressures of inner growth, the effort to
keep in equilibrium the pairs of opposites and then relate
this process as it exists in your own life-pattern.

Recognize, at the same time, that it is only at the lower,

more material levels of manifestation that these pressures are expressed in the many conflicts which cause evil, disease and tragedy. This is at present inevitable because man cannot control his own reactions and does not understand his own real needs. But it need not be so once he learns to obey the great cosmic laws.

Later I will try to show you how, even on earth, the causes of so much imbalance leading to your own ills can to a great extent be eliminated.

Meanwhile I suggest you persist in trying to relate these ideas to your own economy.

For here activities are taking place analogous to many of those in which man and nature engage upon earth. In fact the whole of history, of the evolutionary process, repeats itself symbolically in you. As you know, your life from the moment of conception is, in a sense, a recapitulation of the major trends in development of the life of the race and corresponds also to those which take place in the natural world, the body of the planet. In you wars are being fought at cell level. Your every function proceeds at the cost of the death (the change) of many lesser lives while perpetually within you others are coming to birth.

Now you will realize, if you give the matter serious thought, that each aspect of life must, in a certain sense, be a centre of consciousness since without it some degree of this response to stimuli, however subtle, would be impossible. I do not, of course, imply that the cells and organs of a body are possessed of self-consciousness, only man possesses this; but rather that a power is inherent in every particle which produces its capacity to conform to what, symbolically speaking, is a definite "instruction" or an inherent pattern of growth. This is not a purely biological statement. The law of cause and effect from the past must not be discounted.

This capacity increases as the form grows more complex through the pressure of what are called evolutionary forces, the inner nature of which few understand but which might be thought of as the emergent will of God. This continues until it expresses itself in man as self-consciousness, an enlargement of capacity which can proceed to infinity or, perhaps it would be more accurate to say, to a state of union with its originating Source.

What I am describing is, of course, no more than a faint intimation of far deeper realities, an attempt to express the fact that there cannot exist a truly *separate* entity throughout the entire scheme of things, either in respect of the relationship of cell to cell, man to man, planet to planet or of universe to universe. All are in each and each is in all. Thus the apparent and very convincing state of separation experienced by man is fundamentally an illusion caused by his lack of capacity to see beyond the multiplicity of forms to their common essence and their common interdependence.

This basic condition of unity is being increasingly proved by the scientific discoveries now being made at every level, so it should not be too difficult for you to accept and to apply it also in a personal sense.

No one can escape from this unity—his greater body of Life, the extension of himself in space and time and most certainly beyond; for it is only when freed from the trammels of space and time that man, if but for an instant, realizes what he IS in himself and what his potentialities are.

Nor can he ever break the subtle threads by which he is bound to the rest of the universe. And when, in his ignorance, he attempts to isolate himself he brings upon himself and his world a reaction which produces nothing less than retribution. He is now beginning to discover this as he increasingly exploits his fellow men as well as nature for his own selfish ends.

Look back on your own life and your absorption in self and you will see how true this is.

B

It should become increasingly clear to you as you examine these concepts that, just as to insist on absolute segregation, on complete independence from all other forms of life, would be to perish, so the same law must apply inexorably at all levels, physical, emotional, mental and spiritual. To attempt in defiance of this basic unity to isolate oneself in any way must bring deprivation and therefore some form of death; for some part of the being is thereby being starved of essential sustenance.

This is the reason why all teachings based upon truth insist that it is only through participation, that is to say the establishment of right and harmonious relationships within his own being and with the outside world, indeed with the cosmic laws, that perfect health, happiness, indeed the very fulness of living can result.

If you still question this assertion, study life as a whole and you will soon discover that practically all disorders, not only those from which the human body suffers, but those which appear in greater and smaller centres of being, owe their origin to some act, voluntary or involuntary of non-cooperation.

This may merely manifest as a fundamental inability on the part of some cell or individual to adapt to the rhythm of the group to which it is affiliated; or it may be the effort of one unit to grasp in excess of its capacity for proper assimilation and distribution. Or again it could be due to a determination to retain for the separate self such energies and aspects of life as should be shared with other units with which it forms an inseparable whole. For giving and receiving must complement each other in order that correct balance may be achieved.

No unit—be it a cell, a man or a nation—can live in health and consequently in harmony until this balance of giving and taking is rightly adjusted.

The whole process of evolution consists of a long series or attempts at such adjustments between positive and negative forces, those of activity and inertia. At the lower levels it manifests as conflict between those elements which inhibit change or attempt to oppose progress and those which press against this negative resistance and seek to overcome it. Thus strength and greater understanding should be born. At higher spiritual levels this effort to adjust balance is a form of creative activity; it is essentially co-operative, a choice between the good and the better in full awareness of values involved and is aimed at the emergence of even wider aspects of divine manifestation. Consequently conflict there, as that word is understood on earth, does not exist.

Even among men progress can be and sometimes is achieved without violence given right understanding, but as yet it is only too rare.

The above applies also, remember, to your own small personal world. One could say that illness, in the final count, is nearly always the consequence of wrong choice and aims, lack of understanding of what man is here for, and in consequence lack of balance.

Keep this always in mind; meditate upon it; look back on your own life in the light of this new knowledge and try to see its application in all that has happened and is still happening to you.

The divine laws are inexorable. Effect, however long the process takes, must follow cause. Every action must give rise inevitably to its complementary reaction soon or late.

This law, which maintains an overall balance of forces throughout the universe, is called in the East the Law of Karma. It is the governing factor in the process of reincarnation.

I suggest, until I speak to you again, that you consider the nature of the forces which regulate the exquisite adjustment of part with part by means of which manifestation proceeds.

Is it not through the action of that nucleus of divine creative energy which lies hidden, an undying, inextinguishable spark of Divine Fire, within the core of every living thing?

Look down the years for the manifestations of this creative energy. Is it not this Spark which, burning unrecognized within you, has kept you alive through all your disappointments, sorrows and sickness? Is it not this same purposeful activity, the will to be and to become, which has urged you on in the search for healing, for fulfilment, for beauty, for happiness—in other words for a more perfect expression within you of *Itself*?

And have you not again and again frustrated its purpose by misusing energy in the service of the separate selfhood?

This will-to-perfection is, of course, working through all beings, but the majority are either unresponsive, moving like sleep-walkers, as in a deeper sense they are; or they oppose the divine will with the human will as you have done. How could the result be anything but disaster?

It is only when man is sufficiently harried and harassed by the unanswerable questions his suffering arouses, that he begins seriously to seek answers and the search begins which will lead him to the way of release which all men will ultimately attain.

Such vague discontents, nebulous desires and longings, that cause much of the restlessness which is afflicting humanity today is a sign that there is an awakening to a desperate necessity, the nature of which is as yet unrecognized. It is the stirring of an awareness in man of his true need, his divine potentialities; intimations of that power, glory and beauty which is his birthright if only he can learn how to claim it.

Like a precious seed its potent and revitalizing energy lies in the soil of the human heart awaiting the moment of recognition, of quickening. Yet like the seed, while it is deprived of its rightful sustenance it cannot come to fruition.

Have you not yourself hitherto deprived this seed of what it needs—spiritual sunlight, life-giving rain, by living a life essentially inturned and utterly self-interested, states analogous to the action upon a seed of the dark, dry earth which inhibits growth?

But you can begin to change this condition if, from this very moment, mentally but even more imaginatively (for the imagination is one of the most creative, therefore divine powers humanity can possess) you start to meditate upon the nature of the unified structure of Life in which all aspects of being must play their destined part if fulfilment and happiness are to result.

Such a meditation will evoke within you the spiritual forces of renewal, for in this way you will be making an attempt at last to align your conscious life with the divine purpose.

Do this, not only by trying to see with the inward eye, but even more by trying to *feel* yourself as a cell in the totality of Life, of divine Being.

You will then better be able to judge whether or not you have ever hitherto made a genuine effort to obey these divine laws. As you continue to examine your past life with no self-justification, no excuses and with real integrity, you may begin to understand the reasons why the regenerating powers of life have failed hitherto to operate within your personality as well as upon it from without. Then at last the process of quickening that waiting seed in your heart may begin and the first stirring of a new life will be experienced.

III

It is quite natural that you still find it impossible to grasp that life throughout the universe is an absolute unity; so do not blame yourself. As I said, this idea is particularly difficult for those who have always identified themselves as closely as you have done with the interests and desires of the personal self.

As you learn more about the nature of the One Life and begin to glimpse the significant role which every apparently separate aspect has to play, realization of some of the deeper implications of this concept is bound to increase.

All I ask of you now is that you should endeavour to keep it always at the back of your mind and try to apply it whenever possible to every situation.

Today I intend to speak of one of the most important factors in the process of healing at fundamental levels.

Of all the inhabitants of the earth man alone has the potentiality to become cognizant of his own specific goal and his place in the overall pattern of evolution. In consequence he alone can develop the capacity to unite himself eventually in full consciousness with the divine will.

This is possible because he possesses within himself that centre or nucleus of spiritual light and power of which I spoke in my first talk. This can enable him, when he reaches a certain point in his development, to begin to manifest a host of other powers latent at the various levels of his total being, until he attains eventually to almost illimitable heights of knowledge, wisdom and enlightenment.

This centre is man's Higher Self or Soul.

Much has been taught and written about the Soul, for in some understanding of its nature and function lies the key not alone to man's own being but to the very purpose of his existence.

The difficulty here again, is that in the attempt to define anything of so numinous and spiritual a nature, it is inevitable that words are bound to concretize and consequently to falsify it.

Yet unless there is some understanding of the relationship between personality and Soul, healing at a deeper level can never truly be accomplished.

So I will give you what can be no more than a few hints, ideas, indications about the Soul in the hope that, by meditating upon them and trying to intuit much that cannot be accurately expressed, you will be enabled to take the first important steps across that gulf of darkness which still divides the majority of men from a recognition of their real nature.

One of the greatest problems which confronts the beginner is to reconcile the dichotomy which appears to exist between the idea of a higher and lower level of a man's consciousness—that of the Soul and the personality.

The individual feels himself so completely cut off from this part of his total being which, while it is said to be the very mainspring of his existence, yet seems so definitely "other", remote, utterly detached from all that he thinks of as himself, his feelings, hopes, desires, actions, experiences, qualities, capacities; in fact from all that he *is*.

However often you may be assured that you and your Soul are in essence one, that it is an extension of yourself in another dimension, the assertion has no reality and little value while there is no conscious link with it.

The fact that I have used the word "It" for the Soul tends at once to create a false image in your mind. But if I said "you" that would create an equally false image since you do not feel It to be you. Yet to speak of "your"

Soul is equally wrong for in actual fact I should speak of
the Soul as *you* and the personality with which you
identify yourself as no more than "your" shadow. For
that is exactly what the personality is—a shadow, a
partial projection, an aspect of your real Self. However, I
shall continue to use the word "It" for the Soul, because
this is more impersonal in the sense that it expresses an
individual entity which is neither male nor female, but
contains within itself the experiences and attributes of
both.

But it is absolutely vital in order that healing or wholeness can take place that a serious attempt be made to
realize that the Soul or Higher Self is your real Self,
that part of you which never dies. It is *you,* the traveller
through time, in whose consciousness are stored all the
experiences which have made your personality what it now
is, the qualities and potentialities, the total equipment with
which you came into incarnation. But more, far more than
this: it is the power-house of spiritual light which will
increasingly illuminate your pathway in the world.

Making a short affirmation each morning might help
you to realize this identity of life and purpose existing
between Soul and personality.

For instance try saying with conviction as soon as you
wake:

*I and the Soul are one. I—the Soul—will use the personality
this day in love and service:*

or:

*That which I think of as myself is an instrument for the Soul
to use.*

By making the attempt always to see yourself here on
earth as a channel by means of which an ever closer
communication can take place between you on earth and
the divine powers transmitted through the Soul, you will

be opening yourself out to the greatest healing force in the universe.

So remind yourself constantly that this personality which so often constricts, binds and thwarts your desires and aspirations and colours all your conscious acts and thoughts is no more than the swathes of matter in which the true "you" has temporarily clothed its bright form in order that greater experience and knowledge shall be gained in the material world and greater qualities and powers be developed. This aim also includes the payment of ancient debts contracted in the physical form, since these can only be paid while consciousness is largely anchored at the same level. For one of the chief objectives of the Soul is to redeem poisoned substance by adjusting unbalance, purifying it and creating channels through which enlightenment can be transmitted into the world.

Or think of yourself as its messenger, its partner and co-worker. At least do so at first, until you can acquire the ability to feel yourself and your Soul as in essence *one*; until you know that this centre of wisdom and of pure love *is* you, and that it is only because of lack of spiritual development and true insight that you, here, this temporarily severed portion on earth, are debarred from recalling your true nature and being able at any time to make contact with it. For, remember, contact can only take place provided you create in your personality a channel of communication.

Perhaps an analogy can help you.

Your personality might be likened to a diver who, having descended into the depths of the ocean, is overwhelmed by that mysterious element and becoming entangled in its snare of weeds and rocks loses, in his bewilderment and terror, his memory of how to manipulate his safety-line and put himself in touch with his comrade to whom it attaches him; forgets even how to control the apparatus with which he is clothed and in his panic is threatened with destruction.

Yet you, the diver into the ocean of the senses, the deeps of the seas of illusion, can never be in such mortal danger. For you are never as completely cut off or abandoned as you may well believe at times. All the while your companion, your true Self, waits above you, as it were, listening for your signals. But until you make the effort to pull the life-line and get into communication from your end little can be done that you can be aware of.

There is a correct technique for all activities, spiritual as well as material, and certain conditions must obtain before the Higher can reveal its presence and act within the lower by penetrating the denser layers of matter which separate them. It also is bound by the laws of its own sphere.

So until the diver regains a measure of self-control and recalls the methods he must apply in order to make contact with his companion, he will continue to wander in the darkness and be a prey to the monsters of the deep —doubt, fear and a sense of isolation.

This technique for making a direct contact with your higher aspect of Self is what I shall hope to teach you.

The process must be started from the level of the personality; first, by acquiring a clear perception of the nature of the Soul, then by working to remove the many obstructions which ages of error and blindness have erected between the personality and its progenitor, its own special "father in heaven", sometimes called its guardian angel.

There is a close correspondence here between the work of the personality and that of the Soul; for it is itself the reflection or partial projection of a still higher centre of divine manifestation, a point of spiritual energy whence it draws its own life and being. It, too, is attempting to make contact with states higher than itself, to spheres of greater light and power, its own "father" and its own "angel", in order to be enabled to mirror their image in itself and so project a gleam through itself to you, its representative in a more restricted state of consciousness. And to this cosmic process of transmitting or stepping down the Light from one level to another there is indeed no end. The story of Jacob's ladder is a perfect analogy of this mode of the interpenetration of matter by the revelation of Divine Mind throughout manifestation.

Now perhaps you begin to see why the importance of an ever closer alignment with the Soul is stressed by all spiritual teachers and not for the sake of the individual alone. For every advance towards a closer linkage between this great hierarchy of forces increases the flow of redemptive power throughout the entire network. That is why it is so vitally important for each individual to play his part by working for inner cohesion and harmony in his own small personal kingdom since without these the flow of power is blocked.

To the extent in which you can open yourself out to this inner source of strength and wisdom I can promise you that as the contact becomes closer and more frequent, you will no longer be such a slave to your sick body, the desperate desires and confusion of the emotions and the tensions by which your mind is beset.

For fear and self-doubt, two of your chief enemies, will lessen as you come to rely more upon the guidance of the Soul by recognizing it as no longer an unapproachable "something", separate and remote.

But as I have already warned you, do not expect such a reorientation to take place quickly. It must be a slow process, as is all true and permanent growth. The plant which is forced by artificial means is always weak and easily succumbs to attack. The first attempts must be difficult, particularly for those who have lived hitherto encased in the shell of the separative personality. The shell must be broken and that cannot fail to be a painful process. But you can comfort yourself with the thought that at each crack the Light will be enabled to penetrate more deeply. So meet the inevitable strains with confidence in the knowledge that they are actually indications of release.

Remind yourself constantly that you are no longer alone but united to all other aspects of divine manifestation, and that the "Light within" as the Soul is sometimes also called, is actually a living aspect of yourself. To the extent that you succeed in holding these ideas in mind life will become progressively easier. So many of man's agonies, his fears, his desperate inarticulate longings, his mistakes and crimes against himself and others are due to his conviction of isolation, of being a child crying in the dark.

Because he does not know—for he is so seldom taught—the real significance of his life, he acts always on the assumption that he is on earth for the attainment of purely personal ends and desires. It is only very gradually, perhaps after many essays in living, that he realizes that a life dedicated to these promptings and hungers of his lower aspects of self leads to disease and to general disorganization at all levels of his being. There are still too few physicians and healers who have learned that the real need is primarily to teach man how to make contact with that source of true understanding which can alone be attained at spiritual levels, for only here can the guidance be found which can lead out of the maze in which he wanders.

It is probably more difficult now than at any other time to reach this understanding, for the modern trend is to concentrate almost exclusively upon material activities which shut out the sound of the still, small voice of the true Self, except for those who have attuned their inner hearing to its note.

So begin by seeking silence. Withdraw whenever possible into periods, however short, of solitude and quiet particulary when the voices of your fears, doubts and desires sound most loudly. By attempting thus to still the restless mind you calm at the same time your emotions which are stimulated by the churnings of lower mental activities.

When you, here in the depths, are enabled to recall your own spiritual powers and take hold of your lifeline then there will always be response. Each time you affirm your essential unity with this centre of energy you create an ever stronger channel in subtle matter by means of which help is enabled to come. Eventually you may, in this way, attain to moments of conscious identification with your own higher level of awareness, then you will be enabled to step boldly forward to meet whatever problems and trials may confront you.

For remember: to bring an increasing realization of truth into the lower mind is one of the steps which must be taken eventually by all mankind. This is the cause of that urge which drives man towards expansion, knowledge and discovery. All these lesser adventures are but symbols representing their spiritual counterparts.

Use every opportunity, therefore, to bring down this knowledge of the unity of life which, at higher levels, you already possess.

Open yourself out to every impulse coming from the Soul and so learn to transcend the barriers of the senses which obstruct your efforts to identify yourself with the universal Spirit of which your Soul is but a reflection.

For it is this conscious union with the One Light for which you were created and your heart will never rest, your mind be at peace, nor the lower turmoil be stilled until it is accomplished.

IV

I HAVE already stressed the value of withdrawing from the daily activities for a few moments in order to think about the various ideas we have been studying and trying to see how they can be applied to current problems. But more than this is needed if you desire to make a closer contact with the Soul.

In order to be able to enter at will into the "place of peace" within the heart, some knowledge of the techniques of meditation is essential.

The early steps were taught as a matter of course in all religions in the past. But nowadays, at least in the West, it is more often outside the orthdox faith that teachers are to be found. Many self-styled experts in the art of meditation and in advanced yoga practices attract ignorant people who seek, whether they realize it or not, power rather than spirituality. These put themselves in jeopardy, for irreparable damage can be done if the motive is wrong. Even sincere seekers who try to run before they can walk can be in for trouble. Early steps in meditation must of necessity be slow for the ground must be consolidated at every stage.

The first essential, especially for anyone who is ill, is to learn how to relax. The importance of this is recognized now by increasing numbers of physicians and psychiatrists, for nearly everyone in the present stage of civilization is constantly in a state of tension. Those like yourself who are highly-strung, apprehensive and beset by personal problems find it at first almost impossible to achieve the necessary attitude of calm withdrawal from the general turmoil. But like everything else it can be learned.

So to begin with you should try to put aside a short

time every day—only a few minutes will be enough to begin with—for relaxation.

Try first to relax the body tensions, each limb and muscle. Teach yourself to do so by breathing rhythmically, though never more to begin with than breathing in for a count of two, holding it for one, then out again for two. This is important for advanced breathing exercises can be dangerous unless they are done under the eye of an expert. The real importance is to try as you breathe to give yourself up to that which breath signifies—the regenerating forces of Life. So draw the life-force into yourself; see it circulating harmoniously throughout your whole being, then breathe it out as a blessing, as light, life and love to all the world. This is essential because everything that exists belongs spiritually to the All, so nothing must be held and retained for the separate self alone.

Realize while doing this short exercise that every atom of which the air is composed is actually a spark of the divine Life and therefore should carry, if rightly used, the powers of healing within it.

Let this divine Life interpenetrate your substance by offering yourself to it fully.

Permit no thought of resistance anywhere to impede the flow of these particles of vitality which, while omnipresent, cannot do their perfect work where barriers of doubt, fear, or any form of rejection are raised against them.

Next seek relaxation of the emotions, that is to say of desires and fears and of those reservations and resistances which exist in everyone although they may not be recognized.

This attitude can best be attained by acceptance of yourself as you are, of others as they are, and of all the difficulties with which you may be faced during the coming day. This really means attempting to offer up the human will and desires to the will of the Divine, which is always for man's ultimate good, thus placing yourself, others and even the events of the day at the disposal of higher and wiser powers than you can yourself invoke.

Try, at the same time, to realize that all things are moving towards ultimate perfection, however much appearances seem to contradict this. Realize your own unity with this movement, see yourself as an intrinsic part of it.

As deeper understanding and experience become faith, so such an exercise in complete relaxation and dependence upon the divine will transmitted to you through your Soul must inevitably initiate a process of integration and thus of healing at every level.

By following these exercises with regularity you may begin to feel their beneficial effects in all your activities and relationships sooner than you think possible.

But again, the beginning is bound to be difficult because you have as yet so little control over yourself. For instance you will find that, no sooner do you attempt to raise your consciousness in order to concentrate on any of the ideas I have suggested to you, than vagrant thoughts will crowd into your mind and inhibit the relaxation you seek. The control of idle thoughts, of the normal process of letting the mind wander over the affairs of which daily life is full, is one of the first tasks facing the beginner. What makes it especially hard to achieve is that nearly all such thoughts are bound to be charged with powerful emotional content which itself tends to produce tension.

One thing you must never try to do is to banish such thoughts by the exercise of the forcible human will, that is to say by opposing them violently, even with annoyance. This attitude only increases the tension because it creates inevitable conflict with the desires and habits of the body.

Ways must be devised which do not bring the emotions

into play. There are many methods which will help bring about a condition of quiet and each individual must find that which works best for him.

But one often advocated is to try and look with detachment upon each thought as it arises, relegate your consideration of it until later in the day, then let it slip quietly away after placing it, so to speak, into that living stream of the divine movement towards perfection which should be the final goal of every thought and every action.

Indeed your guiding line in any form of relaxation, concentration or meditation (the three preliminary stages of achieving a closer unity with the Soul) is the attempt to relax into the enfolding power of the divine will. This alone can resolve all fears, conflicts and doubts.

What is essential in this endeavour is never to give up in despair because it does not seem to work and you cannot feel any results even when you have carried out all the instructions. How can you expect to reverse the trends and habits which have dominated you, not only in this life but in very many others, in a few months or even in a year or so?

But every effort you make is having its effect, strengthening the qualities indispensable to ultimate success, for each effort *does* invoke into your being the powers of the Soul.

One of your aims should be to accustom your body and mind to adopt with increasing facility a condition which might be called dynamic receptivity. This is to counteract any tendencies towards passive mediumship. The mind must remain attentive, fixed upon a concept or an idea, never allowed to become blank or empty.

As you continue you will find that you are enabled during the most hurried day, even in the midst of the uproar of the city or the stress of the home, to sink into a momentary silence behind or within the turmoil about you; to retire, if only for a moment, into your secret pavilion, raise to your parched lips the life-giving draught of peace and so renew your strength.

And never say that you have no time to cultivate what is one of the most precious of gifts—this ability to draw aside and renew your spirit through contact with that stream of power which can always bring tranquillity and strength even in the midst of the most violent onslaughts.

Time is yours to use; it is not man's overlord.

Learn to organize yourself and the hours which have been given you to use, wisely and well.

By so doing you will help to train your body to adapt itself to wiser rhythms than those to which it has been accustomed.

Five minutes in the most hurried day can—and indeed must—be set aside at the very least; although the time should be increased as greater facilty is acquired. But even those few minutes rightly utilized could radiate life-energy into your whole being, making you stronger, more purposeful and more resilient. Yet see to it that it is the right kind of energy drawn from the right source, that of the Soul, and dedicated to the divine purpose and not to the desires of the separate self.

The best time to practise this form of spiritual healing is first thing in the morning and a few moments before sleep.

When you awaken, stretch every muscle of your body just as animals do, for they act instinctively in harmony with inner laws. Do this several times, relaxing completely in between. Then breathe, drawing mentally the vital air of morning into the furthest recesses of your being. While so doing dedicate yourself to the Lord of all things from whom alone come the regenerative forces of light and love. Feel them pouring in through your Soul and affirm to yourself that they can lead and guide you in the solving of every problem, in dealing rightly with every crisis, in acting wisely and with love and understanding in every relationship throughout the day.

You might also try visualizing yourself as a little point in the all-embracing Light; a small, bright flame burning within a greater, clearer flame, the radiant flame of divine love.

Enlarge this little point of flame by an act of imagination, see it blending with the Whole.

Use what words you will, for many people need words to stimulate imagination. Or use no words at all. I have spoken before of the importance of this inner faculty of *seeing and feeling* one's way into a concept. So try to see and feel your way towards higher levels of consciousness, free from all those preconceptions, human ideas and prejudices distorting and discolouring the rays of pure light which should irradiate the confused darkness of the realms of dense matter.

Naturally each individual in his daily exercises must find his own special way to invoke the regenerative forces of life. As I have said more than once, words are never at best more than symbols, and symbols stand for different concepts to different people.

But as you have asked for a form of words which could act for you as an invocation and help to stabilize both mind and emotions, I suggest you try using this mystical mantram or prayer which should be suited to your particular needs and temperament:

O benign spirit of love, perfect solvent for all that is inharmonious and impure, this day I offer myself to your service.

Make of me a more perfect instrument that I may become worthy to transmit through the dense matter in which I am embodied some particle of the divine Christ spirit to my environment.

If I do anything or think anything that is contrary to the spirit of truth and harmony, may you, my true Self whose dwelling place is my heart, sound out a note within my brain which may so vibrate through my being that I, here, recognize its warning and am recalled to obey the purposes of my Soul.

When I forget you during this day in the stress of living, recall yourself to my wandering mind so that I may make contact with you again.

May love be my only guide this day; may all my acts be gestures of praise and gratitude, my thoughts be messengers creating in my environment beauty and joy and peace.

Bless my endeavours. Guide my steps. Inspire and strengthen me in my resolutions.

Help me to equip myself for wider service.

I offer this day to you, O, Lord of Life. Fill my Soul with light and possess utterly both It and me.

V

I KNOW that in your heart you still feel that the springs of love, hope and joy must be tarried forever and that it is in any case far too late for attempts to carry out my suggestions to have any real effects.

You also feel that it is too hard a thing to ask of anyone so racked by pain and filled with despair to find hope or comfort in many of these ideas which appear to you, in the main, too abstract and remote to be of any practical help in the alleviation of your condition; nor can you even wholly accept the validity of some of them.

As I have said before, it is bound to be difficult at first for anyone like yourself who has always been so deeply identified with concrete and material problems to believe, for instance, that there could exist within each individual a centre of radiant energy and of potential help; or, that even if it did exist its influence would be capable of working miracles. While to suggest that you could ever feel yourself to be an integral part of the total divine scheme of existence seems totally unreasonable.

Let me repeat: I do not expect that at your present stage you should blindly accept any of these statements. How could you? You have been for too long sunk in what I might call a veritable sea of negativity.

All I ask again, as I did at the beginning of the treatments, is that you should try to remain open-minded and give these ideas a measure of intellectual consideration. Use them as themes for thought. Treat them as theories to be proved true or false as you go along. Try them out; apply them to your problems; see whether or not they work.

But do not overlook the fact that in some form or another

these or similar concepts constitute the basis of the teachings of all those experts, the great saints, sages and teachers, chief among whom were the Buddha and Jesus. These men and women proved to their own satisfaction that *they did work* by basing their whole lives upon them. And it may help you, too, if you realize that all these great ones walked, at some time or another, down the same dark valley that you are now treading and so were identified intimately with the pain, frustration, despairs and doubts common to all men. Yet eventually they proclaimed their conviction that it was this very valley which was the gateway to the glittering heights of realization and illumination.

It is because such forerunners experienced the darkest hells into which man falls that they left behind them all the signposts found in their declarations of belief, in order to point the way to liberation.

For the Path to release from all human torments is one, though the paths to this Path are as many as the men who travel in search of happiness.

But if you still remain convinced that somehow you must be fundamentally different from what these travellers were when they commenced their long journey in search of Truth, then I suggest we return to an analogy I have used before.

Imagine a seed possessed of human reasoning lying in the cold, dry ground. Would it not despair seeing around it nothing but thick darkness, feeling the weight of the soil pressing in upon it, lacking all life-giving light and air, warmth and moisture? Would it not say to itself: "I am as good as dead; there is no hope for me from without, no life to give me power from within." Yet in that seed there exists a potential of energy of unimaginable strength, an aspect of that same energy by which the universe itself came into being. It is this which can make the seed grow eventually into a perfect flower, a glowing fruit. When the fires of spring, the time of renewal dawns, permeating all living things; when moisture penetrates to where the dry seed lies, then Life stirs within its heart; then even in the place of darkness, unseen, unnoticed at first, the miracle of regeneration, of resurrection and rebirth can begin. Frail roots strike down, drawing up nourishment from soil which previously seemed merely a threat to its existence. At last a pale shoot bursts the dry husk and slowly yet surely grows, pushing its way up, forcing the weight of soil, even of stones aside, defying the darkness.

Test for yourself and see the inconceivable strength the life-force possesses when it is stimulated to action. Nothing can resist it. Somehow it will force its instrument to reach the light. And once the shoot has pierced the earth or found its way round a stone and the powers inherent in the light have fallen upon it, greater and greater energies operate to strengthen and beautify the growing form, creating colour, texture, flexibility. So it unfolds and expands, increasing in diversity of shapes until the flower appears; the flower becomes the fruit and in time the fruit scatters its largesse of seed for the forces of life in due season to recharge anew.

This analogy of the seed, as everything else in nature, is filled with spiritual significance so far as man's life is concerned and indeed beyond it. Jesus used it, as did many other teachers.

For the parallel here with the spiritual growth of man is so close. During long ages the forms with which he identifies himself may continue to be apparently unresponsive to the power within, hopelessly imprisoned in the density and darkness of matter, filled with frustration, rebellion, pain and despair. But once he begins to realize that within him is the Source of all life and tries, however feebly to invoke it, the forces of renewal, of love, and the divine will for regeneration focused in the Soul begin to create a ferment within the crucible of his being which, as he co-operates can, indeed, change all base metal into gold.

Just as in every seed the potentiality of growth, the pattern of all its processes of earlier development may be said to be implicit, indeed to be mysteriously "known" to it, so within everything that lives there exists a similar knowledge of its origins and the goal towards which it strives imprinted within the "heart"—a governing intelligence, an inbuilt "memory" of the unique purpose for which it was designed, its ideal archetypal pattern.

This is what is called the evolutionary urge. In the ancestral root, mysterious and dark, knowledge—if it can so be named—is implanted. In the most rudimentary and primitive forms it seeks to mould the dense, recalcitrant matter to that image. But in man this urge towards an as yet unrealized goal is of a different nature, for it is the basic will for conscious union with his primal Source. This never for long permits him to rest. It is veritably the Hound of Heaven.

It dwells within him centred in his Soul which is as a messenger voluntarily descending into form ever seeking to draw its shadow upward to a realization of his own divine origin.

To man the promise was given: *Ye shall be as gods, knowing good and evil.* It was not the devil, but Lucifer the Light-bringer, symbol of the forces of enlightenment, who thus enticed man to arise from a condition of mere consciousness of being and commence his long journey into illuminated self-consciousness. For only through knowledge of the darkness can the urge come to escape from it and the Light be recognized and invoked.

This experience is being forced upon humanity today as never before, for never before have his mental faculties been so stimulated nor his consciousness of his separate selfhood been so acute.

The future depends upon how many can be aroused

from slumber to start on the journey, even as you are now doing.

Remember that man's goal, in spiritual terms, is the purification and trans-illumination of substance.

For as still, clear water mirrors the bank without flaw but when ruffled by a breeze or polluted by mud and slime gives back a false image or no reflection at all, so the archetypal Ideas, symbols of divine laws, can only be reflected into man's consciousness through media which are themselves luminous, harmonious and pure.

The task of all Intelligences, teachers in and out of incarnation, and everyone who, still struggling in the turgid waters of earth-life has glimpsed the possibilities of greater wisdom and light, is to help humanity calm the conflicting currents in its own nature so that truth may be revealed.

This can only be accomplished by each individual attempting to create in himself a centre of harmony, purity, rhythm and, above all, of love and compassion. You, too, will eventually be enabled to act as a channel through which the redemptive forces of the divine Life will be enabled to penetrate the darkness of matter and stir in their winter sleep the seeds of regeneration.

One of the greatest difficulties encountered by those like yourself who are at long last beginning to make a contact with your Soul and to listen to its voice, is that at first its tones are bound to be so confused, indeed often distorted by the voices of those unruly forces which are a part of the personality and have hitherto exerted great influence upon it. They are rebellious "little lives", the many still powerful and separative aspects of the self related to past phases of evolution. They represent all the deeply implanted habits, beliefs and attitudes springing from fears and prejudices. They are still living forces buried deep in the subconscious, often created during many lives. Any determined effort to integrate them with the rest of the personality arouses what is, in effect, a defensive attitude of self-preservation for that would mean loss of power—a form of death; so they fight to retain their separate existence.

This is something that must be recognized and dealt with, for while these forces lurk in the depths they will never cease to present a serious menace to your every effort to make links with your Soul.

This lack of unity within yourself is one of the main reasons why it is so important for you to understand your own nature and to be able to recognize these recalcitrant elements when they try to take charge, for they have a far greater destructive influence upon the health of the personality than beginners realize, and to be ignorant of their nature is to easily become their slave and their victim.

Help coming from a genuinely spiritual source is often obstructed by these forces in the subconscious because it is so difficult for the sufferer to discriminate between their clamour and the whisper of that "still, small voice". This is one of the reasons why the wisdom of this indwelling "god", although present in all human beings, still remains generally ignored or stifled.

So many of your present troubles are due to the barriers you have built in this and other lives between these lower and the higher aspects of self caused by concentration upon the fulfilling of your desires and personal interests at the expense of those of others. Added to this is the expenditure of energy—and remember that energy is divine—on irrelevancies.

To recognize and to accept this is already an important advance, so do not lose heart.

In order to change this situation a pause, however short, when you are planning any activity connected with the daily intensive preoccupation with your own material activities, would help you acquire a more rational sense of values. For by means of such moments of detachment you would be more likely to be enabled to see your intentions in the light shed upon them by your Soul. A regular attempt to do this would be a real step towards acquiring the ability to act always from a higher than normal level.

Eventually, as you persist in this exercise, more and more barriers will go down within your divided self. As water wears away a stone, so each effort to reorientate yourself will weaken those forces in you which block the inflow of the light.

It was you who originally gave them strength and let them become your master, so obviously it is now you, personality united to and strengthened by its higher counterpart, who must dissipate all that stands in the way of true, self-conscious union.

This cannot be effected by the action of any outside agency as some religions teach. Only you, that is to say the divine in you, can redeem you from your errors, although it is true that many outside agents can "point the way".

Setbacks and initial failures are often responsible for the abandonment of the quest for wholeness of being.

Because the struggling personality cannot see any results for a long while, indeed often at the beginning seems to find himself in greater difficulties including increased physical reactions, he decides that it is the teaching which must be at fault. But it is of the utmost importance to realize that directly a genuine attempt is made to change the whole orientation of the life there is this resistance of the "little lives" to be reckoned with, and it can be tremendous. But so long as you remember this, you will not be unduly discouraged.

Every journey begins with the first step and the first step away from this servitude to the forces of ignorance and enslavement to what are, in effect, the primitive powers of ignorance, is by making the determined effort of which I have already spoken, to examine impartially all the diverse elements in one's own nature. This implies, of course, a readiness to face and to accept anything, however disagreeable, that may come to light.

For self-knowledge is the key to self-mastery. Many doors open to him who has achieved control over the forces of his lower nature—those giants upon the threshold which seek to prevent him from becoming lord in his own kingdom.

When you can achieve this it will not be a triumph for yourself alone; if it were so, would it not be but another form of self-interest and separativeness? For since man is indeed the microcosm of the Macrocosm, it follows that when the individual acquires true power of government and control over this one small aspect of universal life—himself—and begins to understand the true purpose of manifestation he inevitably acquires at the same time a greater capacity for wise government in wider spheres of activity and so fits himself eventually to serve the Whole by playing his part rightly in the world.

But to attempt to rule his small kingdom without first understanding its constitution would bring disaster. This is the basic cause of most of the tragedies and failures small and great which befall man in his 'inner' as well as his 'outer' spheres of endeavour.

In order to study objectively your own nature you must attempt to look upon yourself *without self-pity, without fear and without resentment*. For by judging yourself and your reactions as you might judge those of a stranger, with an unemotional, detached and even ruthless examination of motives, you will actually be attempting to acquire the vision of your Soul which always knows the truth about its personality, as the veiled eyes of the separate self can seldom do.

To abandon every rag of self-deception, every specious

excuse which cloaks truth, is essential if you would be clad in the new robes of health and happiness.

This attempt is particularly difficult for those who have lived for long with false images of themselves. Indeed it may be impossible until a certain number of illusions have been first cleared away.

So if you mistrust your ability to look honestly into your heart and to lay bare your most hidden motives —and very, very few are capable of this though many believe that they are—then go to one who loves you greatly and wisely and bid him show you a picture of yourself. Or if you have not merited such a true friend, go to your enemy and listen open-minded to his criticism without instantly defending yourself against it. But if you have neither friend nor enemy go to a wise and tolerant priest or a physician or anyone who has a deep understanding of human psychology and ask for truth.

The vital importance of such a search is to prove to yourself that it really is truth that you demand of life. So watch your reactions. If, when criticism arises there is instant rejection and denial, then you can be sure that somewhere the arrow has struck a vulnerable point. Try to examine it. Meditate on what you are told and ask your wiser Self for guidance. Never hide your face from either your faults or your failures. Failure can, indeed, be your greatest teacher, it can reveal an as yet unrecognized weakness if you use it as a mirror into which you can gaze without fear. Even your enemies who reveal your faults to you in malice are doing you an invaluable service.

I know that you are inwardly ready and capable of taking these first difficult steps of clearing the ground. So, as you continue to try and do your part in what is an essential preliminary to any process of lasting cure, I will endeavour to do mine and help you unveil the mystery of your being, the secret of your true needs.

For I repeat yet again that if a patient does not himself

co-operate and attempt to play his part in healing this breach between the higher and lower aspects of his being and endeavour to integrate them in a unity of purpose and of love, a cure, even if it were to be effected, would not be of a lasting nature. It might enable the patient to live longer, thus giving him the opportunity for greater experiences and wider relationships essential to growth. But apart from this it would achieve nothing but a temporary removal of what, in fact, are always indications of a more deeply hidden disorder or some extensive field of unbalance or ignorance which the action of the Soul may be attempting to bring to the attention of the personality. For unless such disorders are dealt with they cannot fail to manifest again either in the present life or in another in a similar or different form of disease which might even have become, through neglect of the lesson they were designed to teach, greatly intensified in the interval.

So when what men think of as "Fate" strikes, either in the form of misfortune or sickness, the wise ask themselves: "What is this designed to teach me? What is my true Self trying to show me? What must I do to be healed?" Only they can find the answer.

Take this thought with you to meditate upon until I come again:

The Soul is true lord of the personality and its many aspects. You, here, are designed to be the Soul's messenger clad in garments of flesh for a little while in order that you, the part, may learn to unite with the "Whole" in order to find true fulfilment.

For that "Whole" is more than the Soul. This is itself also only a reflection of higher aspects of spiritual Being. It constitutes a link between "earth and heaven" by means of which the shining Sunlight of regeneration could be transmitted to each individual seed still buried deeply in ignorance. The personality, therefore, is ideally the instrument whereby the significance of love and light can penetrate the darkness and confusions of the lower worlds. So, as each unit succeeds in uniting itself with its Progenitor, increasingly the Light will blaze forth into the earth and transilluminate the darkness as it has done through so many messengers in the past. But only when all men become at last channels for the Light will every living thing share in Its mysterious and unutterable bliss.

VI

It is indisputable that self-consciousness must be the first step towards God-consciousness. Therefore, since all the great teachings affirm that God-consciousness, that is absolute identification with the will and purpose of the Creator, is humanity's ultimate goal, it follows that it is towards increasing consciousness of all aspects of himself that man is destined to progress.

This is why it is of primary importance that each individual should make every effort to understand his own lower nature, since it is at this level that knowledge of his higher self is obstructed.

We have already seen that in order to know yourself you must learn to look at yourself "without self-pity, without fear and without illusion". For these three hindrances to clear vision represent some of the most formidable barriers to greater advance. They are children of ignorance, sources of much of man's spiritual blindness and lack of wisdom. They also represent some of the more destructive of the elements humanity has fathered and are among the most difficult to overcome and to transmute since they are the very quintessence of separativeness and therefore the direct antithesis of the fundamental aims of evolution.

Self-pity is one of the most inhibiting forms of separative thinking and feeling. Its influence begins to diminish once some measure of realization dawns that all life is one organic whole. For then the individual begins to see himself no longer as a separate unit destined by some malicious and inexplicable fate to suffer in a unique way, but as part of a closely knit community of lives, a cell in the body of humanity just as humanity is a cell in a far greater community of cosmic Intelligences.

And when he also begins to realize that each unit has made its own destiny, has chosen deliberately at a higher level to work out its specific life-pattern, his sense of grievance cannot but diminish. More, once he can accept that what he is and does can make a contribution to the ultimate purpose of the whole, the value even of his sufferings and failures begins to be seen as part of the total process of healing and redemption.

But you have not reached that stage yet. You find it interesting as a hypothesis and even at moments convincing, but of little practical use while you still fail to *feel* this unity with humanity and lack, above all, a personal sense of commitment.

Even when you are working with others you retain this inner conviction that somehow you are different, isolated in some way through having experienced, as you like to believe, many more frustrations, failures and illnesses than they have. Consequently you tell yourself that you will never be in a position to provide a contribution of any value to a wider scheme of things. This you resent and so pity yourself for your handicaps.

Can you not see that it is because in the past you have refused opportunities and persisted in an utterly negative and uncooperative attitude of mind which still dominates your outlook, that you have remained so deeply immersed in a *sense* of isolation? It has been said that: *As a man thinketh in his heart so is he.* And until you begin to change from this constant dwelling upon the idea of being somehow ill-used by fate and start applying the teaching which has been given you to your situation, affirming it again and again when these moods of bitterness seize upon you, you will be definitely inhibiting the very possibility of the opening out of wider horizons for which you hope.

It is never easy to realize, when one is so deeply involved in it oneself, that the main cause of all human misery lies not so much in circumstances as such, but

c

rather in the *attitude* of mind with which they are met. Yet this has been demonstrated often enough.

Some people who are victims of overwhelming catastrophes in their private and public lives yet meet them with equanimity, wisdom and even cheerfulness by keeping a sense of proportion and of true values. The majority make mountains out of mole-hills because they do not possess this ability and cannot set the events of their lives in the larger context of their whole contemporary world. By making the attempt to identify themselves imaginatively with all those other millions who have infinitely greater trials and agonies than they have ever known, they might begin to see how fortunate they are instead of ill-used and arbitrarily condemned to sorrow and loss.

By pitying yourself and dramatizing your troubles you are actually, although you may not realize it, increasing their power over you. You are opening yourself out to their destructive instead of to their educative aspect. And, although you may not believe this, one part of you is enjoying such an attitude which gives it a feeling of importance, a spurious sense of superiority in the belief that its sufferings are so much worse than those of others. What it is really doing is hugging ever more closely the rags of self-delusion.

Every time you do this you are identifying yourself with what is, in essence, one of the greatest of all illusions. By relating every experience exclusively to your own small separate self, its desires and presumed deserts, you are taking up a position which strengthens that barrier which you have built between you and the creative aspects of Life itself. And since this attitude cannot be indulged in for long with impunity you are actually calling down upon yourself the inevitable consequences, forms of physical and psychic isolation from the Life-force which *must* eventuate in further sickness, neurosis and other ills.

Looked at from this more comprehensive angle suffering is seen to indicate and to reveal (if the patient is ready to open his eyes) a condition of resistance to or non-cooperation with the Soul in its attempt to gain relative balance between the forces incarnated in its vehicle of manifestation on earth. Balance is maintained by means of rhythmic cycles in the natural world; but man no longer obeys such rhythms. So he is incapable of following corresponding ones at higher levels. If he could do so he would move, by initiating the right balance between the opposing elements in himself and society, to free and enlightened co-operation with the whole of life and exist in a state of harmony.

Because he is intrinsically one with his world, Life, in various ways is always giving him signals, warnings, directions. You would be wiser if you concentrated more on attempting to recognize your personal sufferings as messages which must be deciphered in order to discover what it is Life is trying to tell you about yourself; a far more useful occupation than bemoaning your condition.

Compare all experiences, good or bad, to waves of a river upon which you should allow yourself to be borne out of the stagnant shallows into the great creative sea of divine intent.

There is still a strong element in you which resists the tides of growth and change. And until you begin to recognize and accept the deeper purposes behind all that happens to you, these great waves cannot carry you effortlessly and joyously out of the silt and over the rocks. Only when at last you succeed in abandoning the painful struggle you wage against the irresistible tide of the divine can a great many of your troubles end.

At the moment, despite a widening of vision and increasing understanding, something in you often deliberately avoids applying the techniques you have been taught to deal with difficult situations. When this happens remember the warning I gave you about the inner resistance of those "little lives".

To change the metaphor. I often see you as a dancer who, having hitherto refused to learn the steps of the dance and being unable to understand the rhythm of the music, is not only dancing out of step but is also attempting to move against the stream of the other dancers on the floor of life. So, besides creating chaos among those nearest at hand you are inevitably buffeted, trodden upon and roughly treated, for which you blame everyone but yourself. Neither the music nor the dance is necessarily at fault, but only the dancer who refuses to learn.

This analogy, partial as it is, applies to the majority of those who are unable to adjust themselves satisfactorily to life and find relationship with others too difficult to achieve. They are not truly interested in their fellows but only in themselves. They blame life, the laws of the land, other people's bad behaviour or lack of understanding, anything and everything but their own shortcomings.

What is urgently needed, particularly at this phase of evolution, is a more general realization of the fact that much of the suffering around and within each individual is simply due to a total lack of understanding of what real harmony implies. Very few can see that right relationship between part and part, right balance in the handling of energy, of giving and receiving, in short, the practice of what in essence is *love* is the answer to every problem.

Only when this is more generally accepted as a way of life will true health—which is essentially right balance—be attained.

This period of search for answers to the questions aroused by the general condition of chaos in which you, and indeed all humanity, are submerged at the present time, is an inevitable stage in the travail of the soul of mankind. Out of the dark womb of ignorance it is struggling to reach the light, blindly like a babe which is born through pain and effort. Man, too, is but an infant in understanding, but he is being forced, by the stirring of the divine within him and his world, to move forward towards new revelations of truth.

This is bound to precipitate suffering because there are in man so many opposing elements, particularly those of inertia which always fears change and resists it.

These birth-pangs are beneficent, but can only be recognized as such once he sees them in essence as liberators, as teachers, and remains alert, aware, interested, ready to learn, to search for their inner meaning and significance.

Surely you can see now that to waste time and energy in self-pity, in bemoaning the present and endeavouring to project yourself either into the past or into an unknowable future, is not only futile but actually harmful; being essentially negative and uncreative it holds you back from growth and renewal. What is more, it can be dangerous as it could worsen your present conditions; for this refusal to live fully and positively in each moment as it comes and in seeking this kind of escape can cause a form of atrophy to set in at some level of the being which could easily result in disease or a state of weakness preventing the accomplishments of the specific tasks for which you came on earth.

The objective of your Soul is that the personality should learn certain lessons which it has refused to learn in previous incarnations. If it fails yet again, this will inevitably create new conditions of conflict which are bound to make the lessons harder to learn another time. The consequences of continued refusal can be cumulative. If it occurs too often, a life of such misery is produced that in despair the personality is driven to seek, as you have done, for guidance out of his darkness.

Now perhaps you begin to realize how important it is

never to try to escape from any experience or any set of obligations which come to you, but rather to learn to interpret their message.

So from now on try to view your sufferings in the way I suggest. Seek to understand what your Soul is trying to show you about yourself and your real needs. At the same time realize that if you accept these birth-pangs and live through them with courage and intelligence they could bring into existence as yet unrealized powers and qualities—those potentialities hidden still in the higher regions of your being for which you, in the personality, have never as yet provided any means of expression.

It might help you to see your present difficulties as analogous to those tests and trials which the aspirants in the past had to experience in the temples of initiation but which are now being undergone by means of the day to day difficulties of living in an age of exceptional stress. For such trials of patience, strength and courage are always essential before progress beyond a certain point can be made.

But you must also not lose sight of their value in that process of which I have spoken so often, the redemptive aspect in which the whole of humanity is destined, one day, to play its rightful part. Since each individual has something he was created expressly to accomplish in this total plan, you should try to discover what your contribution is meant to be; what specific colour you should be painting into the shining multi-coloured picture represented by humanity; what type of thread you are called upon to weave into its tapestry; what note is yours to sound forth into what may often seem to you the cacophany of modern life but which is, in truth, merely the as yet distorted transmission by imperfect instruments of the music of the spheres; what your own place is in the movement of the dancers upon the floor of life.

You, in your higher Self know the answers to all these

questions. So when your state appears to you to be particularly meaningless and uninspiring, your colour drab, your note harsh and out of tune, remind yourself that this is only because as yet your eyes are not open to the part you should be playing in the delicate and complex pattern of the Whole, and set about remedying this by practising the techniques I have taught you.

Until you achieve some measure of success you must just accept this phase as one which is obviously needful and is therefore valuable, if only to induce you to turn to your Soul more often for enlightenment and thus attain to a deeper and more penetrating state of understanding.

I know you find such an attitude at times almost impossible when the darkness and depression seem too profound to be dissipated by any means whatsoever.

But think for a moment; is it not true that in order that forms (which are exteriorized ideas) can become visible to man's restricted vision, darkness is as essential as light? How else could light be known except by contrast with the opposite? In the same way the good, the true and the beautiful in order to become real to man as he now is, are only recognized as desirable states because of the effect the impact of their opposites, evil, suffering and confusion has upon man's consciousness. What is more, these are the spurs, the slings and arrows which arouse him from apathy and indifference and stimulate him to seek escape by exploring the potential strengths in his own being.

This progressive endeavour to discover the mysterious roots from which truth and beauty emerge into his chaotic state to transilluminate it, will lead him to find the means by which he may express such divine powers in himself.

Instead, then, of being sorry for yourself you should be rejoicing that you are not so handicapped as the majority, since in this life at last you have been forced by fate to recognize your own ignorance and helplessness and so have been driven to ask to be shown a way to remedy your deficiencies.

You must not get the idea, of course, that such a change in realization will automatically free you from suffering either in this or other incarnations. How could it? Even if it were so radical that your whole orientation to life became miraculously altered, it would still need to be tested and this would necessitate meeting many new as well as old familiar experiences in new ways dictated by your newly acquired insights. Which means that the effects initiated in the past through ignorance would still have to be met, lived through and transmuted before all imbalance and weakness in body, mind and emotion could be totally eradicated. But as greater understanding and spiritual alignment develop you will find that you are enabled to meet all such tests effectively so that no new sources of what might rightly be designated in this context as "infections" would be generated.

What is more, it is only by developing the capacity to pass creatively and with understanding through all the vicissitudes of life that higher qualities *can* be developed.

It should by now have become obvious that the only means by which those like yourself who have hitherto felt themselves to be prisoners of adversity can break away from such pessimistic and negative states of mind, is to recognize and accept that adversity is, or can be, always a true friend in a harsh disguise once it is recognized as such. I advise you to try to see, in future, every event which appears to be shattering your life or forging shackles about your eager feet as, in reality, part of the process of liberation.

Gethsemane need never be the end of all hope for a fuller life of greater opportunities. It may, indeed, be the one way of bringing the victim out of its tangle of weeds into a far wider freedom and a clearer light than he has ever known, once he can be persuaded to seek the path leading out of that dark garden. But this can only take place when he can say to that divine all-seeing Light within, "Thy will be done".

Such complete acceptance is, of course, one of the most difficult and yet one of the most essential attitudes to be acquired by those who would walk this path of healing; and it must be a positive acceptance based on understanding, not a hopeless, negative acquiescence. In fact only real understanding can make it possible. Ideally too it should be one of gratitude that a new opportunity has been vouchsafed to practise a fresh approach to life in order to prove its validity.

Too difficult? Of course it is at first, and will be even for a long time. Now you may believe it to be quite impossible. I assure it is not, given patience and practice.

It will be particularly helpful here to remind yourself again of the natural rhythm of growth which must be slow in order to be firmly established.

So long as the desire to grow and develop spiritual faculties is there, that is enough to begin with. The realization that nothing comes to you without due cause, that nothing is fortuitous or arbitrarily imposed from "outside" should also help.

Increased understanding of the working of the great, universal Laws should also enable you to realize that in a deeper sense your "enemy"—the adversary to your peace who thwarts your desires—represents always, at one level or another, some as yet unredeemed aspect of yourself. So in every such encounter you will gradually be able to discern what particular weakness is being revealed. Try to see each as a catalyst which could cause some new truth to emerge and welcome it as a friend bringing a gift.

Eventually, if you persist in this endeavour you will be able to receive calumny, unkindness, injury, ingratitude as you would receive gold, and the harsh words of a critic will be of more value to you than the flattery of a friend. By abandoning pride, which stands nearly always in the way of the acceptance of truth, you will begin to view even your worst enemies, be they persons, situations or what is called "fate", as your greatest benefactors; they will be recognized as agents sent to help you develop the spiritual qualities of forgiveness, understanding and, greatest of all, a sense of compassion for the blindness and ignorance of humanity which is always causing injuries to itself.

The tragedy is that so many valuable gifts and opportunities are rejected by the personality because they do not take the specific forms it desires. Very few are capable as yet of discerning the true value of experience and reading the secret message it is sent to convey, so they miss the chance of extracting gold from what appears to be only dross.

For this gold—which is truth—is always hidden in the most ordinary experiences of life and can be extracted from everything that exists. It will be offered to man again and again until he has learnt to discern it with the open eye of wisdom and discrimination and has come to accept whatever comes to him eagerly, seeking only to discover of what spiritual power this particular gift is the symbol and the harbinger.

Naturally at the beginning of your quest you are bound often to fail in what is an exercise of perception, for it is one of the most difficult to develop and even many great exponents of the religious way of life have still much to learn in what truly is a great art.

But however often you do fail there is no need for self-condemnation or a feeling of stress or anxiety. Indeed the beginner who expects or demands too much of himself, sets his standards far beyond his present capacity, tries to force himself to behave like a saint long before he has even set his feet on the hard road leading towards perfection, is most likely to be suffering from a dangerous form of vanity—that of *hubris* which the Greeks believed was always punished by the gods. And what are the gods but the forces of evolution?

Realize that defeat and failure do not matter as much as conventional human thinking makes people believe. They can, if we try to decipher their message, represent "a finger pointing the way", what Christians would call the hand of God; but only if a man has the courage and wisdom to search for their deep, hidden roots. For in these roots lies the true cause of the flaws in character which make defeat and failure inevitable.

At present no more is asked or expected of you than the attempt to recognize every opportunity for increased understanding which experience offers to your evolving consciousness. Set yourself honestly to discover what you can learn from all that happens to you, good or bad, and what it can reveal to you about yourself and your world.

Perhaps now you are beginning to perceive the possible reason why the cure of sickness is not always "permitted" to take place? The personality is not learning the particular lesson sickness has been sent to teach. For being, as so much illness and tragedy is, a symptom of a deeper state of disharmony and unbalance, should a cure take place before this deeper cause had been recognized and eliminated, the personality would only have to experience similar disorders at another, and perhaps not even so propitious a time.

If the aim really is to attain a lasting state of health, such an intelligent attitude of understanding and acceptance must be cultivated.

You can encourage yourself by keeping in mind that by every effort to cleanse these infected roots, whatever strains this may inflict upon your personality, you will be eliminating the causes which have brought you to your present state. You will also be creating harmony in the conditions surrounding you. I have emphasized before that as this atmosphere within and outside becomes increasingly purified and stabilized, it will attract to you forces and powers you have never, in this life, been enabled to contact and these will be yours to use in future in far wider than personal spheres.

But this will depend, of course, on whether you are wise enough never to forget that they must *not* be used for purely personal ends.

The appropriation of divine Energies and Powers which, remember, are expressions of living Beings, for the benefit of the personal self is in fact a form of black magic although of course it is not generally recognized as such. More troubles afflicting man today than you would believe arise from this misuse of what should be considered a sacred trust. It brings inevitable disaster because it is perverting and in consequence poisoning aspects of creative substance. This will infect subtle elements which will be re-embodied in the make-up of the personality in future lives, if not in the present one, and will continue to influence him until he himself succeeds in purifying them.

You have committed many such sins in the past which are the cause of some of your present troubles.

Begin now, therefore, to act in such a way in the ordinary affairs of daily life that the process of purification may be hastened by the transmission of harmony and happiness to your environment. Seek to forget your own pains and depressions in helping others. So you will progressively open the channels through which your Soul can send its healing benison of radiant light, not to you alone, but to all those with whom you are drawn into relationship.

VII

WE have attempted together to understand some of the causes and effects of self-pity and have recognized not only its futility but the dangers of indulging in it; today we will consider the nature and dangers to the psyche of fear.

Fear is a condition common to all humanity and perhaps the greatest cause of damage to physical, emotional and mental health. If you do not believe this try to analyse the weaknesses, errors, habits, beliefs and powerful desires with which the average man is beset and you will be amazed to discover the part fear plays at every level, in how many forms it manifests and the shapes in which it masquerades, also the influence it has on the way in which individuals react to experience.

Fear with you, as with the majority, is still the charioteer who guides the horses of emotion, mind and will and more often than not breaks the chariot upon the rocks of ignorance. Until control is taken out of his hands and his power over you is dissipated this erratic and dangerous course will continue.

Clearly, then, one of the first things to be done is to learn how to take the reins into your own hands, or rather put them into those of the true charioteer, your higher Self. When you can do this, even to a small extent, you will be capable of making servants of your fears, that is to say use them only as and when they could be useful as indications of danger and no longer crouch helpless under their dominion, a victim to their negative, destructive influence.

In order to do so it is first essential to discover to what an extent fear has gained control and where it is most powerfully entrenched in your being.

One way is to examine carefully the nature of your actions and reactions. You will soon discover how few of them are quite untinged by some shadow of fear—remembering always that vanity, desire for success and approbation and many such apparently unrelated urges often have fear as a basic motivating cause. Such an exercise will prove to you the extent to which fear must be outgrown before you can rule triumphantly in your kingdom.

I use the term "outgrown" advisedly; for while I would impress upon you that at the present time fear is one of your chief barriers to progress, I do not imply that fear has not also its rightful place as a beneficial agent in the development of a large proportion of mankind. As always everything depends upon the stage at which the individual stands.

It is obvious that at primitive stages (and these exist still in many people who consider themselves to be advanced and civilized, for the "savage" and the "animal" are seldom as far away as the majority would like to think) fear is still essential. Fear has impelled man to develop some of his most precious gifts and has even given impetus to many great reforms. It also saves him from activities which are self-destructive and can arouse whole communities from complacency, apathy and deterioration.

But there comes a stage in man's development when fear must be superseded by love and wisdom, together with a recognition of the existence of those spiritual forces which, if invoked in the right way, can guide every individual in his activities more surely than can the blind and primitive forces of the past.

Fear is a definitely separative tendency. Whereas this at first makes for individuation, once that is accomplished it becomes no longer constructive but destructive. As man advances in awareness of the necessity for co-operation he also grows in his comprehension of the essential unity of the Whole. Then fear is seen to be a danger to the forward movement of evolution. Thus comprehension begins to dawn in the human mind that what is valuable—even essential and therefore "good"—at one stage of evolution can become "evil" or at the very least obstructive when a more advanced stage is reached. The value of all phases (or teachings) is relative according to their use as incentives or obstacles to man's advance.

But within man as yet nearly all stages still exist and exert their influence upon his behaviour if only as dreams, subconscious urges or shadowy memories arising from areas of the subconscious life which belong as much to the whole race as to the individual. It is from these, as well of course as from the natural and right urge to self-protection that innumerable fears arise.

So it would be absurd to suggest that even an individual who considers himself to be highly evolved should eliminate all fear from his composition, for fears will continue to manifest and to exercise their powerful influence over man's actions until he has reached a stage where the influences which dominate him come predominantly from the Soul. Then a truer spiritual perspective and sense of values will place him beyond their power.

This is the stage, although most of them are unaware of it, towards which all those seeking happiness and fulfilment are aiming; a stage incompatible with the dominance of the hosts of fears now ruling humanity. But as man increasingly succeeds in recognizing and obeying the voice of his true Self fear will gradually be absorbed by the influence of those higher forces which evolved men are capable of contacting and manifesting.

But for the majority this day is far off. In the meantime disease, sickness and disorders of all kinds multiply as fear in a world which grows ever more violent and competitive causes the individual to feel himself increasingly insecure.

So far as you are concerned, until the beneficent elements in your nature have grown strong enough to eliminate the worst ravages of this enemy to your peace it would be well to discover means by which fear can at least be controlled and perhaps also in some degree transmuted.

For a large number of people like yourself who are excessively sensitive, nervously over-strung and even partially psychic, the present age is a particularly difficult one. Their reactions to the shock waves of collective fear, to the supercharged vibrations of emotion, anxiety, resentment and violence which are sweeping the world can be at moments almost unbearable and consequently are bound to affect adversely the etheric body. This, of course, causes similar reactions in the organs of the physical body. It is thus all the more necessary that such people should learn how to protect themselves from this ceaseless bombardment.

What you need is to acquire safeguards which could greatly mitigate these threats particularly to your emotional balance.

I suggest that, in the first place, you should try to realize how much time and energy which could be put to more constructive use and employed in strengthening your body and calming your mind, are wasted through the anticipation of situations, misfortunes and failures many of which may never materialize. The use of imagination in such negative ways is a normal concomitant of fear. So many of the things people dread and which, in consequence, weaken their resolve and their fortitude, become powerful emotional blocks which prevent positive action and influence their response in advance to opportunities and situations when they arise. Not only this, but they create mental pictures or thought-forms, centres of energy in more subtler matter, charged with the negative force which gave them birth. These can actually affect the atmosphere with their emanations and so influence any who come within their orbit. This of course applies equally to thought-forms of a positive and optimistic nature.

It is not often in any case that the future resembles the terrible things so many people in their moments of acute panic or gloom fear regarding their personal life. But if such thought-forms are constantly created and brooded upon they can become so charged with magnetic force that they tend to draw to their creator the very experiences he dreads.

So remember, when you make persistent pictures of your inability to deal with any given situation or problem, that you are actually injecting into it negative energy which will tend to create the climate in which your fears are most likely to materialize. At the same time you are diminishing your own powers and abilities at mental and above all at spiritual levels. Yet these powers could also be recharged and strengthened so as to enable you to deal adequately with the situation should it be unavoidable.

According to the manner in which you habitually think, so daily and hourly you are building analogous qualities, powers and tendencies into your character. These must inevitably affect your whole orientation to life. In consequence all attempts to transform negative attitudes dominated by fear and anxiety into positive ones which brace, stimulate and inspire confidence cannot but help you cope with problems as they arise and in time will gradually eliminate the worst onslaughts of fear and despair.

But when you reach a stage of genuinely accepting the existence of a stronger than human centre of energy in yourself which can and should be called upon for help and inspiration, then the whole situation will be bound to alter, for you will know of a certainty that you no longer fight alone.

Until this stage is reached, try to practice habitually the transformation of negative into positive thinking until it becomes a habit. Each time you do so you are increasing your capacity to accept every experience as a challenge rather than as a threat and will be gaining strength to meet that challenge should it come.

But if at present this attempt to exorcise thoughts of fear seems impossible and you continue to be haunted by dread of future events founded, not upon imagination, but upon very definite probabilities such as increased pain, personal loss, old age, an existence bereft of those material things and relationships which seem essential to your very life, then I suggest you try to employ a different technique. Face your fears squarely, for it never helps to hide from or shut one's eyes to what one believes to be inevitable, although, as I will try to show you, even what seems inevitable may still not happen, or when it does may not be as devastating as you anticipate.

It has been said by one of the wisest of poets:

Since the affairs of men are still uncertain.
Let's reason with the worst that may befall.

Having then imagined "the worst that may befall" try to see how such an event could best be faced and dealt with in the wisest possible way; what actions on the physical plane—but far more important what spiritual attitudes—would help you in such a contingency to meet the situation at all levels.

One way to do this is to see the experience as if it were happening to another person. Exteriorize it, detach it from your own specific conditions and above all from your emotional reactions. Consider what practical advice you would give such a sufferer. Imagine him dealing with it efficiently and with common sense. Try to envisage also the inspiration and strength which could be evoked were he to make the attempt to lift the situation into the revealing light a higher perception could cast upon it. But what is also important, imagine him not only enabled to deal with it but gaining benefit from what at first sight might well appear to be an irrevocable disaster.

For instance, think how the experience might actually be turned to good account; what lessons it could teach him and how he could be enabled, by accepting it with courage gain in qualities, insights, moral strength and above all in the ability to help others in like case.

Such an attempt to objectify your fears will enable you to judge the various aspects of the threat to your personality with greater detachment. This is what is needed and is so difficult to acquire. It is always easier to consider the problems of another without bias and illuminated by the clear, penetrating light of truth than to see one's own which are bound to be entangled in the net of personal emotion, fears and hopes.

But when you make such an attempt and have decided upon the best attitude to adopt should your fears be justified, the next important step is to try to put the whole situation behind you. Do not continue to dwell upon it or turn it over in your mind. You have made your decision, that is all you can do. Now leave the whole problem alone. Whenever the thought of it returns, as it is bound to, try to replace it immediately by a confident assertion that, whatever happens, you will always be aided to meet the situation wisely and constructively.

It is also useful to review your armoury from time to time and see what progress you are making in the forging of those spiritual weapons which will be yours to use in all such eventualities.

You may find that none I have so far suggested help

you to any great extent, although it would benefit you to experiment with them.

So let us see if we can find other methods of removing this great pressure upon you compounded of so many elements which from your earliest days have affected your health and cast their dark shadows upon your mental and emotional responses, distorting your whole attitude to life.

We have already considered the tremendous effect that mind can have upon the emotions and seen that magnetism is one of the most potent and creative of its powers.

One extremely important method of dealing with those armies of negative and often threatening thoughts which persist in invading the minds of everyone at times but more particularly those like yourself who are abnormally sensitive to atmosphere and can therefore become the prey of the impact of the universal fears and apprehension which are now infecting the whole emotional climate of the world, is by a deliberate attempt to focus *attention* elsewhere. This means concentrating exclusively upon some specific idea or activity which has no connection with the obsessive thoughts in question.

Attention is one of the most powerful ways of concentrating energy upon some specific focus; for it causes consciousness to be drawn away from all other areas of thought, will or emotion and so injects a stream of power into the new focus. When it can be achieved successfully, awareness even of the existence of the body itself can be temporarily obliterated.

Let us take an extreme case as an example. Such a pain as toothache is normally impossible to forget even for a moment and focuses everything upon itself so that even the fingers can hardly avoid probing at the aching tooth. Now suppose a sudden crisis arises—an emergency, an accident, a fire in the house, a call for help from someone in danger or distress. Attention immediately shifts; all the energies formally absorbed by the pain become centred on the emergency which, if acute enough, can even cause it to be temporarily forgotten or at least greatly minimized because all the powers of the total self are concentrated elsewhere.

Or consider a less dramatic situation such as that of the man who is utterly absorbed in the effort to solve some difficult problem, a scientist, a businessman or someone trying to concentrate on a chess problem. Such people can be so completely identified with what they are doing that they become oblivious to everything happening around them, even to interruptions, noises and sensations of heat or cold.

This ability to switch the attention from one focus to another through complete identification of the personality —and therefore of the energies emanated by it—on some specific point can be of great value in removing conscious-ness from fluctuating waves of anxieties and fears.

So when you find yourself in the grip of some obsessive emotion or mental activity from which you cannot escape and which holds you tenaciously in its grip returning again and again to plague you, try switching your mind in this way to something more impersonal connected neither with the past nor the future but with the here and now. In your case a problem of metaphysics or perhaps one associated with the technique of your specific creative work would serve you best.

Set about concentrating upon it with determination, trying to probe it to its depths. In this way automatically the energy hitherto churning around uselessly will be transferred to this new centre. Tension will be released and balance restored if you persevere. For tension is largely caused by undue concentration of energy either physical, emotional or mental upon some threat or prob-lem connected with the personality.

The common expression "to take your mind off it"

is based upon sound advice and many people do this automatically, unaware of what the actual process involves.

So in future use this method intelligently and with deliberation whenever you find yourself slipping into the old repetitive rut and the pressure of your fears and apprehensions, to which since childhood you have conditioned your whole economy to respond, begin anew to overwhelm you.

This is one of the early methods taught in the technique of meditation; it develops the power to concentrate upon more constructive and remedial lines and can serve you well at all times of stress. It also helps to train your lower mind to be your servant instead of your master.

Another more creative method of removing your attention from your own affairs is to turn it towards those in distress, sending them thoughts of compassion and trying to invoke into their situation the strength of the Soul. For remember, on the planes where the souls of men are most active and aware, there is a far closer unity and telepathic contact than can ever be apprehended by their shadows here.

In the final count of course it is for each individual to work out for himself how best to change the negative vibration of fear into one which is constructive and into which his energies may be directed with greatest effect, to find the specific "escape-hatch" which will best serve his needs, appeal to his temperament and release him from the servitude to those thought-patterns which tend to return again and again acquiring strength through repetition.

This exercise of control like every other new technique, will probably seem difficult to carry out and for those who have never attempted to discipline their unruly aspects of self before, quite impossible at first. It is, as usual, largely a matter of determination and patient practice, but the most important factor is a strong desire to change these wrong modes of behaviour into right ones, destructive energies into constructive force, slavery to the emotions into freedom from all such damaging and debilitating states of consciousness. But try to realize that the very fact that you, in your personality, are now attempting to deal with such inner enemies to your health and your peace, will bring you help hitherto beyond your reach. Your real Self desires as much as you do—undoubtedly far more—the liberation of its shadow still immersed in darkness and overwhelmed by material and psychic pressures.

While experimenting with any of the ideas I have suggested you should also try to hold the realization—and constantly affirm it to yourself—that nothing is as inevitable as it may seem; that a change to more constructive and optimistic modes of thought, combined with a condition of preparedness may possibly be the very means which can be used to avert, to some degree at least, the full impact of whatever it is you fear.

Realize also that by a courageous and eminently practical attitude of concentrating upon the present, instant by instant, rather than spending your time brooding upon a hypothetical future, that is to say by making each moment as perfect as you are capable of doing, you could be in one sense actually modifying the course of the stream which hitherto has been carrying you like a leaf passively towards the event you dread.

To revert to an earlier metaphor: once you learn to take the reins of destiny into your own hands you might even be enabled to direct the horses into a road other than the one upon which you believe disaster must lie ahead.

It is said: "the stars incline—they never compel".

So even if the events you dread are inevitable because they are part of your life-pattern, you are not necessarily compelled to be overcome and crushed by them. For remember, the horses stand for emotion, for desire. Learn to control or at least to modify these, change your concentration upon your personality to reliance upon your Higher Self (the true charioteer) and disasters, if they should come will not have the same effect upon you as they would have if they struck you as you are now. *For they will be met by a different person,* one armed with new qualities who has become capable of meeting them wisely and constructively with understanding and detachment; a person, moreover, who has acquired that spiritual strength which can always be drawn upon once the ability to do so has been acquired.

There is another point you might be wise to keep in mind; the intrinsic importance of any event does not lie primarily in the actual event itself but always in the reactions to it of the one involved.

Concentrate on perfecting this link with your true Self and in time all those fears which now so torment you will melt in its pure flame; then you will know the fulness of joy which is of the spirit and be truly healed because you will "sin" no more.

VIII

TODAY I want to try and make you realize more of the nature of the specific quality radiated from Soul level which can work the miracle of eventually eliminating the basic causes of sickness.

This is love; for love in its full and deepest meaning is a force which can indeed in every sense "make whole". For wholeness implies the integration of every element in the being in a condition of perfect balance and harmony which results in a condition of perfect health.

Love, being the principle of unification, reconciliation and harmony is one of the greatest remedial powers. It is the very root of well-being and the fount of joy.

Love, as a universal energy is rightly identified with the Source of all energies. Consequently the assertion that God *is* love is the most simple and comprehensible way of expressing in human terms the nature of THAT which reveals itself through the highest of all qualities man is as yet capable of knowing.

So we find that love in some or all of its aspects is the centre and core of all the great religions and spiritual teachings.

In scientific terms it is the law of magnetic attraction by which one particle gravitates to another and blending with it produces new forms; in fact it is the force which caused the multiplicity of lives at every level to come into manifestation; that energizing will which is associated with the idea of God as creator of the universe.

It is this same law operating that irresistible and fundamental urge in man that draws him towards unification with his One Source even when he is unaware of the nature of the impulses which activate him.

Another characteristic of love is the quality of self-giving.

In the animal kingdom this essential urge is expressed through sex or by the protective instinct. At higher states of evolution, although love still operates in this way, the deeper nature of love becomes progressively revealed in the measure that man himself becomes capable of showing forth such qualities as the understanding of need, compassion and utter forgetfulness and even sacrifice of self.

Informed by love the individual then becomes as an open door for the flow of archetypal love—the Christ spirit —into material conditions. By this means ever greater understanding of its intrinsic nature is transmitted to humanity.

Even so as yet earthly love at its best is only a shadow of the true nature of this supreme creative, healing and regenerating power. The love of which the majority are capable, that passionate attachment to persons or con- ditions or things, the desire to keep and hold for the separate self—is not much more than a faint shadow, sometimes even a distortion and a perversion of its essen- tial qualities. It can indeed, at the lowest level become, through the urges of self-love, harmful, destructive, evil and dangerous, just as every divine manifestation can be darkened and debased by the shadows of its opposite.

The whole history of humanity can in one sense be written in letters of love if studied with understanding; from that universal form of love reflected through its great saviours which has inspired and elevated those it has touched however fleetingly with its fire, to all the lower manifestations of wrongly directed love that have caused unspeakable sufferings.

The more you meditate upon the influence and the powers of love, the more you will begin to realize that what I first said is true. It is absolutely fundamental—it is the essence of Life itself. There is nothing that it cannot perfect and glorify once its true origin and nature is recognized as the basic expression of Divinity in the world.

If you could perfectly practise love, every inner conflict would solve itself.

Because its essential nature is to unify, it not only has the power to heal, but also to cast out fear. Fear ceases for the man who can wholly identify himself with the divine will-to-good which is but another word for love. This has been proved innumerable times by the power love possesses to strengthen even the most weak and most cowardly. Examples of the effect of love in changing man's whole orientation are innumerable. It has inspired individuals with wisdom and audacity and has enabled thousands to face and overcome with equanimity many forms of danger and disaster, even torture and death or the agonies of sickness.

It is said that in the East where men follow the way of compassion in utter dedication sages have even walked unharmed among the fiercest of beasts.

For that which man fears is nearly always the encounter with an exteriorization of some aspect of his own nature. To him who has wholly tamed the tiger in his heart, the tiger in nature would no longer represent a menace. The radiation of love would be so strong it would bring him to the man's feet to bask in its life-giving force.

If it were possible to manifest the quality of genuine love perfectly in the lower self this would instantly obliterate from consciousness all those manifestations of "not-love" which man is always encountering in his life by reason of the affinities existing between them and their reflections in his own personality.

But only the very few have reached this stage of perfection. Even the best and noblest are still the battleground of contending energies. And as a man allies himself to one or the other of their expression they attract to him magnetically their own affinities in the outer world. Like always attracts like in some degree or another. Fear breeds fear; hate, hate; violence, violence and so conversely. He who loves truly and with wisdom (for this is important) will evoke love and confidence from the most unexpected quarters.

You may point out many examples in daily life which apparently contradict this assertion. Outwardly they may do so but inner affinities will always be found to exist by those whose eyes can see below the surface appearances.

Jesus was acting upon his knowledge of this fundamental law when he bade men love their enemies. He knew that ultimately evil can only be overcome by good and that through loving a man not only creates within himself a centre of spiritual power and inner tranquillity, but at the same time emanates a form of magnetism which can arouse into activity any good which may be latent in his enemy's nature. *When there is sufficient response* this could even cause him to cease from his evil intentions. Naturally in many in whom no adequate response exists, love is met by violent opposition.

Too brilliant a light, too powerful a force such as Jesus and many lesser spiritual leaders emanated, can so dazzle those in whom there exists no answering gleam that they are filled with fear of losing the strength upon which they pride themselves, and this arouses the hidden demons to resist the pressures of love and so generates hatred.

But so far as the average man and woman are concerned there is not likely to be any danger of such a reaction. For the love they are capable of expressing is such a pale shadow of its prototype.

Now let us try to apply these concepts of the nature of love to your own case. Although you have loved and been loved, your own love has nearly always been so mingled with personal desires, so demanding of response, so exacting, that it has defeated its own ends. It has not attracted but repelled.

This has been due in large measure to your ignorance of one of love's essential qualities which is always to release rather than to imprison. By attempting to hold anyone exclusively for oneself his freedom to grow and express his own nature is threatened. In self-defence he fights back and separation, in some form however subtle, is more often than not the outcome. Like again producing like. Fear instead of freedom and joy is the fruit of such love as this.

I have already equated true love with understanding and compassion; this implies a response to another's needs and weaknesses which comes from the wisdom of the heart. It means *accepting them for what they are*. It has been said that "to understand all is to forgive all". Forgiveness, in the true meaning of that term, is the manifestation of the highest form of love.

But to understand others in this sense implies highly developed powers of spiritual perception.

You can now see why I always stress the need to understand your own nature. For without such knowledge you will be liable to project aspects of your personal desires and prejudices upon others, seeing in them what you wish to find, be it good or ill. This very common tendency is the cause of many illusions and tragedies in human relationships. Genuine love can always pierce through the many disguises behind which men hide.

When you succeed in gaining this form of insight as regards not only yourself but others also, you will begin to understand a little more of the need for man to practise increasingly the integrating power of love in all his activities.

But how, you may reasonably ask can this idea of loving all things, even one's enemies, be applicable to the dark side of one's own nature? How can you be expected to love all those unbalanced and still unregenerate energies, the recalcitrant "selves" we discussed earlier, the "demons in the depths", as they are sometimes called?

Let us consider their nature again. We have seen that these forces, lusts, passions and frantic desires, cause of inner turmoil and consequently of illness in virtually everyone at some stage or another, constitute the residue of man's primitive nature, in many ways analogous to the animal and child stages of development, which have not yet been integrated into the whole.

Ideally of course man should have succeeded long ago in bringing these forces under the control of his higher and more evolved aspects, or better still, have transformed them from being his masters, as they so often are, into good and useful servants. But I need hardly tell you that this is very seldom the case.

The reason why you and so many others live in fear of their sudden eruption into activity, usually when the personal will has been thwarted, is that their real nature is seldom understood and consequently they have never been trained as all forces in nature must be trained if they are to re-become what in essence they are, angelic rather than demonaic forms of energy.

Generally speaking early neglect, violent suppression, lack of sympathy and wise training of the growing child together with elements generated in the far past contribute to what amounts to a sundering of these forms of energy from the main stream of development. Being, as it were, left behind, they consequently behave irrationally just as children do who have never been successfully integrated into the family.

This is why you sometimes feel as if there was a definitely alien spirit dwelling in your body—a traitor hidden in your citadel. You fear its moods which affect you despite yourself, casting you into darkness without any obvious reason, even forcing you to speak cruel words or commit foolish and ill-considered actions which another part of yourself condemns. What is worse, the more you struggle with it, seeking to drive it from you by force, the more it prevails.

It is equally useless, to argue with these inner forces, to admonish or command them. They do not respond to reason because they exist below this level and are part of the emotional make-up. You cannot, in the personality, which is so largely in thrall to these lower influences, defeat them in the very realms where they are most powerful.

Violent or stern repression is even worse, for it directs energy into the very aspects you should be seeking to transform. This is one of the most dangerous errors committed by many religious and puritanical fanatics.

A rather similar attitude is taken up even by some so-called esoteric schools. They stress the necessity for beginners to aim at "killing-out" their human desires and weaknesses even their sense of separateness, and to fight *with the will* against aspects of the personality many of which stem directly from subconscious levels.

In the first place the use of the *human* will in any difficult situation of this kind should never be advocated, especially when it concerns the more subtle aspects of being. Man is not yet ready to use it because the human will is seldom or never free from some taint of desire, self-interest, violence or desire for dominance.

Secondly, it is a fallacy to believe that anything can be killed or annihilated. There is no such state as actual death, there is only change, transmutation, growth, becoming—a movement of matter or of consciousness from one condition to another.

This applies to the recalcitrant aspects of the nature as much as to any other state of being. If it were possible to destroy these forces what would be left but a vacuum? And what might well be sent to fill it by the ignorant personality? Jesus, considered by many to be one of the greatest psychologists the world has known, gave us insight into this problem when he spoke of the cleansed and emptied room whence one devil had been evicted and into which seven worse promptly entered.

What then should replace the human will in the attempt to deal with and purify the lower aspects of the nature? What else but the power of love, since it never destroys but always transforms.

Do not fall into the error of thinking that I am suggesting you should love, in your human way, the actual manifestations of these misdirected energies in your life, that you should pander to your weaknesses, pity and act tenderly towards them.

Very far from it. Remember that the word 'love' has many connotations.

What I am saying is that you should first attempt to use love as a method of understanding them. For love always implies understanding. Try to recognize the *essential* nature of these forces which you cannot control as god-given powers which you, and you alone, have perverted and debased because in this and previous incarnations you have had neither the knowledge nor even the desire to enable them to manifest aright since you have constantly diverted their energies to satisfy your desires.

By so doing you have been instrumental in transforming them from "angels" into "devils", from bright, constructive forces into dark and destructive ones. Not only, therefore, should you feel compassion towards them but compunction also. It is for you to deliver these "spirits in prison" to restore them to the brightness which you have tarnished. Until you succeed in doing this you will yourself never attain to the wholeness and joy you desire, for they are part of yourself.

By practising this form of imaginative transformation you are projecting redemptive power into the confusion of these unruly forces. The attempt should also help you to realize that everything that takes on the appearance of evil both in yourself and your world is, in fact, always the result of the perversion of divine energy through its misappropriation by the ignorant human will which has degraded and metamorphosized it.

All such forces must be transformed back into their true purpose and function if man is ever to reach a condition of harmony and this can only come about by a deliberate effort to submit all that has been degraded to the redemptive action of love—as the supreme solvent, the only power that can create permanent harmony out of chaos either in the personality, the state or the nation.

And love, remember, also implies sacrifice. Where love is invoked into any situation, there schism and consequently ignorance and evil will eventually be abolished.

So far as you are concerned this can only be achieved by your maintaining at all times an attitude of awareness; watching your acts and thoughts in order to recognize whenever what I have called "not-love" creeps into them. This means a readjustment of virtually your total response not only to the forces within yourself but to those outside, to your associates and to the world in general.

But above all it means that in every crisis you must invoke the qualities of love by visualizing its energies pouring through from Soul level in streams of living light.

By making the attempt to maintain what is, in essence, an orientation to the Real rather than to the ephemeral (which does not mean non-participation at the material level—quite the contrary), you will be using love to influence and transmute all the recalcitrant forces within your own nature and of course this will have an effect far beyond yourself.

As the Soul is the bridge between spirit and matter, so

D

you, child of the Soul, must learn to act as a bridge between this regenerating light and the denizens of your own dark, chaotic realm and so do your part in ministering to these "spirits in prison".

For most surely the closer you can arrive at identifying your personal self with your real Self and draw upon its higher energies to help you in this work, the more rapidly a synthesis of all aspects of the personality can be achieved.

At the present time this ability to manifest love more perfectly in the personality may seem no more than a remote ideal. But it need not remain so if you learn to cultivate it. Everything you do, the books you read, the kind of music to which you listen, the general tenor of your habitual thoughts, the judgments you make regarding others, the type of energy you put into your work are all having an effect upon your whole economy by linking you either to the lower or to the higher levels of being.

This applies to everyone. The majority of people concentrate their attention in the main upon transient and often childish things, seeing everything that impinges upon their consciousness and relates to their way of life in their short-term and material significance; hence the confusion and the tragic conditions in the world.

If more people could learn to set apart a time of quiet each day in which to escape from the pressures of their existence by invoking the influence of the divine overshadowing forces of love, an extraordinary transformation of the world scene could take place.

You can at least do this. Try, at these times of withdrawal, to feel—yes, and see with the imagination—this regenerating power of love penetrating into the darkest and most primitive regions of your being in gentle and compassionate streams of radiance to where those turbulent forces of ancient error await redemption. For I repeat again love *is* the only power that can redeem and transform evil into good, ignorance into wisdom and disease into health.

Remember the old story of the princess who, to save her kin, voluntarily wedded a ravening beast. It was her beauty, her pity which conquered him. It was her kiss of love that enabled him to cast off the enchantment which had chained him to the "animal" kingdom and freed him to appear in his true guise—a prince, the lover of her dreams.

This is a profoundly symbolical tale as are many of the fairy-tales and legends the inner meaning of which has long since been forgotten.

So when you are in despair try to see these darker aspects in yourself which so often torment you as in essence glorious aspects of the One Life, temporarily bewitched and imprisoned by the spells of the workers of illusion, the forces of ignorance and blindness in the personality.

Work at their release by manifesting in all your thoughts and actions the regenerating powers of love. Thus you and they will eventually be released from your bondage.

IX

WE have been considering ways in which the power of love can be used to control and guide the forces which animate you. But the process must not stop there since the personal self is only a tiny cell in a far more vast complex of beings.

How then can greater cohesion and harmony be brought, not alone to your own small kingdom, but to that greater one also? For this is certain: no single unit can reach perfection itself until it has succeeded in perfecting its attitudes towards all its co-workers, those other human units with whom its life forms an integral whole.

Although this stage is, for the majority, very far off as yet, those few who possess greater understanding have a greater responsibility and should make it their predominant aim. This implies the achievement of greater unity and harmony first in their own small sphere of influence, particularly as regards those with whom they are placed in close association; for they can be sure that they have been drawn together owing to links from the past. Such links could have been of all kinds, but we will consider now those which have precipitated the inharmonious conditions that have become a definite part of an all too common life pattern in humanity.

You have now, through increased understanding, been able to recognize many such links in this present life and the possible reasons for the particular conflicts and difficulties this has created. It has been especially obvious in your involvement with blood relationships, many of which certainly result from ancient antagonisms and injuries inflicted on both sides.

In such cases it is particularly important that every effort be made to create now, in this present life, harmony out of conflict, at least so far as your own reactions are concerned. You may not be able to modify theirs. But that is not your affair; though a change of attitude on your part can have a greater influence than you may know.

You were born in the same family as an ancient enemy in order that both of you should have the opportunity to break down the age-old barriers of hate and resentment and until you succeed you will be fated to meet again until true understanding in one of you is born. That one will be freed from the bondage; the other will have to learn the lessons elsewhere and by other means. But learnt they must be and put into practice. For one thing is sure, the worse you treat each other in the present life the harder reconciliation will be in the future, for evil will generate more evil until you come to your senses and realize that the process must stop. Then wisdom and compassion, the forces of love, must be brought into play to dam the turgid stream and purify it by draining the poison out of it.

Since at some time or another this process will have to take place, you, who have gained some understanding, should make every effort to initiate it now, however hard it may be to break the habit of resentment, jealousy and even hate.

What is very serious and should give all those who churn over grievances grave concern is that wrongs remembered in bitterness act like a canker and are the causes of many physical and psychological disturbances in the system. Psychiatrists know this of course, but their knowledge does not go deep enough, for they are not aware that such attitudes generate a continuous flow of what I can only describe as psychic acid into the etheric and can even affect the astral body. These penetrate the physical body and eventually unless checked can be the cause of many of man's incurable diseases. They also tend to create powerful thought-forms which cause disturbance and unbalance in mental matter and can bring about obsessional delusions.

Unfortunately past wrongs nearly always tend to be recalled through the clouded distorting mirror of man's own desires and limitations; this twists events out of their true shape and significance and causes mole-hills to be transformed into mountains through that common faculty of self-deception with which you all pander to your own weaknesses, desires, vanities and resentments.

I spoke earlier of the value of *attention* in the process of transformation, and pointed out that to focus attention on anything or anyone is to inject into the subject of your thoughts the type of energy which empowers you. This is why any form of negative or destructive criticism should be at all costs avoided. It can have a serious effect at subtler as well as at objective levels similar to those I have just mentioned. So when critical thoughts arise, replace them immediately by positive ones, affirming the good qualities of the one you have been denigrating, the abilities and strengths rather than the weaknesses. Thus you will be helping him as well as yourself, for something in him will be touched and will respond even if neither he nor you is at the time aware of it. And remember the analogy I have used before—the boomerang always returns to the sender.

In any case you should have realized by now that your enemy is only reflecting back at you destructive energies you have yourself created. Once you have eliminated them, his malice will arouse nothing but compassion and the desire to help him.

One of your faults which comes from a far past is that you have never known how to forgive; you may repudiate this, but remember, injuries which have been truly forgiven are also forgotten in the sense that they do not return to haunt the memory; no scars are left. If recalled at all there are no longer any emotional reactions for the poison has been drained out of them.

The ability to forgive in this radical way comes only after many attempts. You may have to forgive your enemy actually unto "seventy times seven" until you have succeeded in coming to terms with the true enemy in yourself and so be enabled to create here at least a creative atmosphere of love.

Until you succeed in this task, there will be no escape from the obligations such difficult relationships impose, for they are, in fact, opportunities presented to the protagonists by the Soul; each ignores or seeks to evade them at his peril.

It is no use to imagine that you will not have to face them at some time or another if you do not do so now; they will return to you again and again until you succeed in transmuting them by the powers of love. Nor will you find true healing and peace until these conflicts are ended.

For although the outer form of the personality changes in life after life, the same unresolved weaknesses, the same lack of balance and more important still, of love, will continue to be re-embodied in each personality you inhabit until they have been redeemed.

Many people deceive themselves by imagining that they will be entirely different personalities in the future. This is a pleasing but erroneous form of self-deception. The basic personality can only be changed by the changed attitudes it takes in the *here and now* and the efforts it makes to acquire greater understanding, wisdom and love which alone can transform the giants of self-will and ignorance into beings of light.

See to it, therefore, that you concentrate upon letting these regenerating forces flow freely into all ancient patterns of conflict in accordance with the command of him who taught that love was the prime necessity for right living, hence for happiness and health. *This command I give unto you, that you love one another.* And he died in fulfilling it.

His way of manifesting love was by making himself at all times a channel for this universal solvent to flow through him into every living thing.

But still the voices even of those who claim to follow him find reasons for rejecting it.

"This command is too hard for us. How can we be expected to manifest this kind of love when we have never experienced it ourselves? How shall we love when, desperate and hopeless, we see nothing about us but hate and violence? If it is true that only through pouring out love to all can our desires be fulfilled; if it is true that until we have learned to love and forgive our enemies we cannot draw love and forgiveness to ourselves, what hope is there?"

But would one who was the breath and fount of wisdom and compassion have mocked men by asking them to do the impossible? By declaring to mankind that love was itself the expression of the divine nature, he gave to the world a new aspect of an eternal truth—that love is the specific form of power which all men must and eventually will manifest because in essence all men are divine.

For all that is emanated by this one creative Source must incontrovertibly partake of its nature; and if the nature of the Emanator men call God, is the very quintessence of love, the expression of absolute unity, it follows that there can be nothing which does not possess the potentiality of manifesting it and so becoming *whole.*

Thus the first essential for all those who are aspiring to transmute the darkness—the expression of not-love— within themselves, is to make every effort to produce the requisite conditions in which this redemptive power can operate and increase.

But while the heart—symbolically its central point of ingress—remains dessicated, proud, egotistical, clogged by self-pity, filled with hatred or envy, in fact profoundly separative, how can it act as a channel through which the forces of integration can flow?

The bud which is prevented from opening its chalice to the sun shrivels and dies, incapable of perpetuating itself through the living seed. So it is with the closed heart. It cannot fructify aright the mind to transform the life, for a mind which remains unresponsive to the power of love deprives the whole body of its rightful sustenance.

It is because of this general condition of "deadness", this lack of the capacity to respond to the light, that Jesus by word and example bade men again and again cultivate love. He knew that only by so doing can suffering humanity attain that "more abundant life" which is true health.

So, if it often still seems to you that as yet no such springs of love and regenerating power exist within yourself, take comfort. They are there. They do not manifest because as yet you have not learnt how to exteriorize them. Start by practicing the arts of caring, service and goodwill in every situation and you will call them into being in yourself as well as in your environment.

We have only as yet considered a few of the specialized ways in which love reveals itself. One of the chief is through creativity. This may seem strange to you, but is not creation essentially a formative and reproductive force? It is not the essence of that impulse of Life to grow, to develop to infinity? Creation is powered by imagination, without which man would never have evolved beyond the primitive state. And is not creation essentially an act of *self-giving*? The artist, the musician, the inventor and the scientist give themselves unreservedly to their work, subjecting themselves to the discipline imposed upon them by that mysterious driving force Socrates called his daemon. And what is this but an emanation from that creative centre, the Soul? So, too, the mother gives her all to the child in her womb and the lover to his beloved.

In this expression of love as giving, we have another interpretation of that saying of Jesus: *To him that hath shall be given.* For in the degree that man possesses the capacity to give of himself so, in that degree, does the power of love grow and develop within him. More, by giving without stint of all he has, he draws to himself greater, more spiritual gifts. Seeking to express the will of the ALL in his small way he becomes, in the final count united with *that ALL to which he gives.*

Let no one declare that giving is impossible, that he has nothing to give. Many, from various motives they seldom recognize, persuade themselves of this. To some extent you have been among them.

They find excuses for not giving. "I am too circumscribed by fate; my feet are bound, my hands are tied; I have had no opportunities to serve others. There is no one who needs my affection. Life has killed my enthusiasms and my ideals. Pain holds me back from service; poverty shuts me away from my fellows. I have no time, I, who am too enslaved by the bitter rhythm of daily work. I have no outlets; I am too old; I am too young; service is too dull and unrewarding. I am too deeply sunk in despair. I am too tired."

There are endless rationalizations which people produce in order to excuse themselves for failure to act compassionately in response to need. Whenever you find yourself doing so, search your heart and see if your excuses are as valid as you would make yourself and others believe.

Who is there so poor, so abandoned, that he cannot find a life in worse case than his own? Go out, therefore, from your dark room of preoccupation with self, and forgetting your own circumstances for a while, look around you for someone who needs sympathy, encouragement, or merely the presence of another who can listen to him, cheer him and give him hope. Help everyone to whom you are drawn into contact. I repeat: "drawn into contact." There is no need, as many people who believe themselves virtuous do, to rush about forcing themselves into, metaphorically, closed rooms. Such determined interference is not actuated by true loving but more often than not by vanity and self-importance or a sense of guilt. But if you adopt within yourself an attitude of readiness, those who need help will feel the vibrations of your heart and will come to you of their own accord. Try silently, using intelligence and understanding to make those around you aware that you are available, ready to meet them where they stand, and to listen. You may not be in a position to give material aid or even advice, but thought and above all that attitude which most people think of as prayer, invoke powers beyond your own and these can flow through you if you keep yourself open to their influence. Even if you are tied to your work, your room or your bed, use this channel which is available to all. Work by using mental matter if you are unable to use matter at denser levels.

All human beings have something to give, some constructive and creative part to play in life however inconsiderable it may appear in their own eyes or in those of others. The man with one small talent would have won his master's approval if he had used it and by so doing developed all its potentialities. If nothing else, you have the fruits of your own experience; let your sorrows and losses be transmuted into wisdom.

Do not concern yourself with the manner in which your efforts may be received. That is not your business. True love is not dependent upon reciprocity. It pours itself out ceaselessly towards everyone and everything within its radius and finds inner fulfilment in this act of Self-expression. For love is its own joy. It arises from an inexhaustible Source dependent upon that alone for its increase, drawing its waters of renewal from a Fount which is limitless.

Such love may be likened to a lamp shining in a dark place. It throws out its beams, regardless of the results of its shining. If no one profits from its light, no matter; it continues to shine. Results do not affect its power to illuminate the darkness around it.

To manifest love at the highest level possible to man at his present stage is so to identify the self with the needs of another that all personal separative desires are superseded. This often means standing aside and not interfering with the other's free will. One of the most difficult attitudes to adopt.

Nothing, neither indifference, ingratitude, change or absence can touch or mar the inner tranquillity and joy of him who has become an adept in this highest and most demanding of all the arts and sciences.

It is, of course, too high an aim for the majority to carry out, for humanity as a whole is still too deeply immersed in self-interest and too closely identified with the personality. But that is no reason why those who aspire to health at all levels should reject it as an ideal to strive for, one, moreover, which is attainable once the Soul has been given greater control over the life.

Because you have been brought up in a country professing to be Christian I suggest you re-read all that Jesus and his close followers taught of the power and nature of love; these constitute some of the most profound and important passages in the religious literature of the world. But you will find that all other great teachers have propounded identical truths in their own terminology for *Truth is one*.

And these teachers themselves proved the validity of their beliefs by practising them. They are witnesses that it is possible to live out these ideals fully in the material world.

There are many people who claim that they "love mankind" or "love everyone"; a vague generalization very easy to assert but usually meaningless. For it is virtually impossible to "love" the majority of your fellow men as the word is generally understood. But remember that it has many meanings beyond those it is given by the average man. Unless love is expressed in action by means of goodwill, some kind of service, harmonious personal relationships, harmlessness, which often consists in refraining from destructive criticism, the claim to love is false. For love is in essence unitive.

Only by keeping this continually in mind can you enable love to flow freely into your total environment and effect those basic changes demanded by him who taught love as the prime necessity for right living in every sphere.

This effort to make love the basis of the life is particularly needful today. Man is putting himself in real danger by his essentially "loveless" relationships not only with his fellows but also with the wider realms of nature. His responsibility is to protect, serve, train and guard the natural world, which he tends to regard as a slave rather than as a beloved child. He forgets that every living thing is an extension of himself in the unified structure of one world, so that there is no part of it which is not also a part of his own total economy. More especially is this the case regarding the animal kingdom with which he is so closely affiliated, for his physical body belongs to this kingdom. Until he comes to realize that by damaging and destroying not only the animals but also his earth out of sheer greed he continues the process of damaging and destroying himself.

I tell you this so as to make clear to you how closely every being is linked with every other. The divine Life animates each and all making all intrinsically sacred.

It is not sufficiently recognized that man has a very special responsibility for the use and direction of this divine Life not only in himself but in the outer world. More, that everything and everyone with whom he makes contact has also an influence upon his own being for good or ill. Everything you touch, see, hear or smell but more especially consume is instinct with this Life and should be treated accordingly as a sacred trust.

You still feel that this transmission of love at all levels and in all activities is virtually asking the impossible. Try it and see. Make an experiment if only for one day or a few hours. By a supreme effort of imagination think yourself into the mind of one of the great ones, Jesus or the Buddha or even your chosen saint or sage; then seek to discover what he would do in your place faced by your specific problems.

Attempt to see the situation with his eyes, the eyes of selfless love; hear with his ears, the ears of compassion; use his hands, the hands of enlightened service.

I dare to assert that if you could succeed in doing this with your whole heart, intelligence and will, honestly and with detachment even for a few hours, you would gain an entirely new vision of the true meaning and purpose of living.

What is more, by adopting this attitude as an exercise from time to time, a definite modification of many of your false attitudes to life would slowly take place and would result in changing your whole self-centred outlook which has done you so much harm.

I would remind you again of the saying that *as a man thinketh in his heart so he becomes*. Thought indeed is colouring, influencing and shaping man's total environment as well as his nature all the time. Thought is one of the greatest formative powers in the universe and until the thinker is rightly orientated to Reality and to divine law it can be one of the most dangerous.

To take one small example: the influence of thought-plus-emotion (for at man's present stage only in a few cases is thought totally divorced from some form of desire) can so charge a room or a place with the type of vibrations emanated by those who habitually gather there that any sensitive becomes immediately aware of and influenced by them. Here is yet another proof of the power of the individual either to enlighten his environment or to steep it in his own gloom or destructive atmosphere. This lays an enormous, if as yet generally unrecognized responsibility upon everyone. You are each continually moulding and creating your environment, and the great pairs of opposites, love and hate, constructive and destructive thoughts, are the tools you use. Therefore all teachers deplore the universal habit of criticism and denigration of others. I have spoken at some length on this subject before but return to it again because people like yourself who are critical by nature find it so difficult to realize the damaging effect it can have both upon you and those you criticize.

So continue to watch yourself carefully. Watch even apparently idle words which could cause pain, distress or induce a sense of inferiority in another, particularly words which are harsh or repressive. Watch even your thoughts. Remember their power to wound or to heal.

It is so much better to refrain from every form of criticism unless it is actually requested; then it should only be given if it is constructive and helpful, for in such cases it can be an aspect of love.

One way of curing yourself of a critical attitude (which so often has its roots in vanity, arrogance, self-importance —even a sense of personal inferiority) is by attempting to identify more closely with those you are condemning and realizing how much they are a part of yourself.

In any case until you are capable of a genuine identification, which is beyond the power of most people, how dare you arrogate to yourself the right to judge another? How can you be in a position to condemn him for his actions, lacking as you must do that insight by means of which alone you would be capable of perceiving their true cause? How can you know the secrets of his life, his struggles, sufferings, disappointments, handicaps and fears? And above all the goal his Soul has determined to reach in his life on earth? In order to do so you would have to become his very self.

If you could actually achieve such insight—which would be impossible until a high spiritual condition had been reached—all condemnation would instantly cease, for compassion would overwhelm you.

What is more, you would perceive that the very faults you had been criticizing were, as often as not, reflections of many of your own. If this were not so they would not have evoked in you such sharp reactions. These are usually signs of an inner subconscious recognition with consequent fear and rejection.

So, until you have cast out the beam from your own eye as Jesus taught, desist from criticizing others and turn to examining yourself instead.

The truly enlightened individual refrains from any form of violent opposition to people, opinions, attitudes of mind, and particularly to anything new, unexpected or even antipathetic to his nature, for such reactions are nearly always powered from the emotional level and should therefore be suspect.

Recognizing that all things are no more than passing phases in the development of the individual or the race, he accepts them open-mindedly with understanding, in the knowledge that he himself has probably passed through many such phases in earlier lives during his long journey through the vales of illusion.

This does not mean that I am telling you to shut your eyes to what might generically be called evil, or even adapt yourself to the false standards of value by which the majority live. Very far from it. You must see things as they are, but at the same time recognize the causes of those tainted springs from which they arise.

This is a sick world just as you are a sick person. But, as I emphasize over and over again, the potentialities for the attainment of health and wholeness exist in everyone, so the healing process must start in the individual. It is from each tiny centre that a reaction can begin which will in time leaven the whole mass.

Perhaps it will help you to be less intolerant if you realize that the evolutionary process, even so far as man's actual form and functioning of his organs is concerned is by no means completed. He is still in a transitionary stage of development. In future ages he will not be a more or less passive agent in the hands of impersonal forces, moulded and governed by primitive powers as he is at present. In one sense he will be consciously his own creator, controlling the processes of his development at all levels by means of contact with his Soul and the creative Hierarchies. Thus he will become ever more capable of building himself upon the ideal archetypal pattern of his Divine Prototype.

By attempting to train you in self-consciousness and self-control I am but endeavouring in a slight degree to anticipate this stage, showing you how you can already play your part in preparing a future vehicle of consciousness in which a greater unfoldment of such potentialities may be possible.

You will find that by keeping these concepts in the forefront of your mind and attempting in all ways to apply them you will be enabled increasingly to participate in the work of regeneration. Try to be more humble and open-minded. Judge less and seek to discern the power of love working under multitudinous disguises and through many unexpected forms then slowly its power will blossom within you and it will flow out from you and transilluminate your world.

X

ONE of your main difficulties arises from the fact that although you can give mental assent to the ideas we have been studying, something in you still tends to reject the belief that you could be cured permanently if you were able to regulate your whole existence by them. This is a reaction from the emotional level and is another aspect of your habitual fear and self-doubt.

But it is essential that you should at least be prepared to experiment with them with the whole of your being, if there is to be any hope of success; and although, as I have warned you often, it could hardly be possible to achieve perfect health in this life, if you can at least begin to resolve the many conflicts still causing so many of your troubles, it would inevitably make a great difference to the remainder of your time here and will certainly give you a far greater chance than you have ever had hitherto of attaining health and happiness in future lives.

So let us call upon a power which stems from a higher than emotional level. Try to use that technique I suggested earlier, the "seeing–feeling" faculty which implies the use of the imagination and a greater power still, that of intuition.

Try to "see" these concepts we have been discussing as living Powers working within and through life in its every aspect from smallest to greatest in a *total* pattern, the movement in time of the manifestation of the divine Will to BE and to BECOME. Realize—*feel*—that since all ideas based upon spiritual perception must point in some degree or another to aspects of Reality, they can, and indeed must, always be recognized as analogues of states beyond anything they may express in human terms.

Do not try, as you tend to do, to work out the validity or otherwise of these fundamental concepts by means of what amounts to a form of mental gymnastics. It is useless. You can only attain to a deeper understanding by a change in the levels of awareness; an effort to use the higher mind which alone can reveal the significance of all spiritual concepts directly, over-leaping dialectic and pure logic, never the means whereby true perception can be obtained. Imagination is, again, the most valuable approach here, for rightly used (that is not allowed to wander off into fantasy) it can lead to the development of that greatest faculty of all—still embryonic so far as the majority of the human race is concerned—intuition.

This is instinct at a much higher turn of the spiral of man's development, and the two faculties are often confused with psychic powers. Instinct is, certainly, a form of psychic sensitivity. But it can be very fallible in man because he has passed beyond the animal phase, where it is of major value, into the lower mental realm. True intuition, direct seeing and knowing, is almost always infallible because it is a function of the Soul. The difficulty for the beginner is to learn to differentiate between the two, but he can only learn as usual by his mistakes. At the stage which you, and the average intelligent individual have reached today, the development of clear thinking is extremely important for it is this which can be used to check anything that appears to come from higher realms but could merely be a reflection from the levels of desire.

You see that here again it is a matter of calling in the powers of the Soul. We always come back to that.

This, of course, applies equally to the resolving of another of your difficulties. You find it almost impossible to arouse in yourself the urge to devote your powers to service by sacrificing your time, your few pleasures, the relatively small amount of energy you have at your disposal.

This ability to give to others cannot be forced unduly, but it will develop as your powers of identification with others increases through the use of imagination and the daily effort to try and seek help from the spiritual forces which are always at your disposal when you identify yourself with them.

As it is unreasonable to expect yourself to achieve unselfishness all at once, at least keep in mind what I have been trying to impress upon you from the beginning of these treatments: that being separative and exclusive can never bring you either happiness or real health. Appropriating that which is in essence universal for the particular interests and needs of the separate unit to the exclusion of others is against divine law, and by so doing you cannot but fail to bring upon yourself increased imbalance, tension and eventually disease.

I can assure you that those who freely give time, energy and talents (all, remember, also manifestations of divine energy) to obeying the law of right distribution, automatically open themselves up to a flow of creative and redemptive power; in consequence they are bound to become recipients of that form of spiritual, mental and emotional energy from which alone peace and harmony in all realms of the being must eventually result.

It would seem you are thinking that this is not always the case.

I would remind you again that situations should not and indeed cannot be judged by superficial short-term human standards. The pattern of life is neither simple nor obvious. There are always causes beyond causes, deeps within deeps which only those with spiritual insight could possibly discern.

In the particular case we are discussing you are overlooking a very important factor.

As man progresses spiritually he has a far greater freedom of choice than his fellows because his wider vision and understanding imbue him not only with deeper compassion for them and their problems, but with a greater sense of responsibility towards life as a whole.

As you know, the choices made by most people are largely motivated by their emotional reactions or deductions by the lower mind. Not many are influenced by true insight and even fewer by a real understanding of spiritual laws.

Consequently the average man is not equipped to perceive the results to which a decision may lead even when it seems at the time to be wise or right.

But it is different with those others in whom the flame of love burns so brightly that sickness, poverty, persecution, even death count as nothing in their passionate determination to help their fellow men.

In consequence many even choose freely before birth to sacrifice all the earthly benefits to which they have earned the right and which most men hold dear, in order to share and alleviate some of the burden which crushes humanity.

This sacrifice can be expressed in innumerable ways; one of the most effective of which is perhaps by demonstrating in their own lives that it is possible to endure far more than the average measure of human ills with courage, patience, even with joy. For it is no matter for comment if the fortunate, healthy and rich are cheerful. But when the light shines brilliantly in one who is struck down by disease and disaster or who lives in poverty in the darker places of the earth, the attention of other sufferers focuses upon him. They tend to ask: "What is the secret of happiness that you possess and we do not? Whence comes this courage in adversity? Share your knowledge with us."

But on the other hand it could be possible that those who have nearly worked out their Karma and are close to freedom should choose, in order to be released for greater work, to pay outstanding debts and experience in one life, all that still stands in the way of liberation.

It is useless, as I have stressed so often, for those with limited human vision and understanding to expect to receive answers to all the problems with which life presents them.

But if you find such suggestions as I have made hard to accept, look back on history. Have not the majority of social reforms and the changes in evil laws and attitudes been brought about by the sacrifices, struggles and vision of the few? If Jesus had not drunk the cup of bitterness to the dregs would he have had the power to draw millions of lost and unhappy souls to him? Would he even have had the right to preach the doctrine of sacrifice of self as he did?

Later I may go deeper into this whole difficult question. But I would stress again that enlightenment regarding the many unfathomable mysteries concerning the meaning and ultimate purpose of man's existence can only come gradually as the seeker penetrates deeper and deeper beneath the outward appearance of things.

All you need to realize now is that every experience has a purpose, and part of its value is to force you and all who suffer to search for it. Sickness, for instance, has been the means by which your own first struggles towards ultimate release from many illusions damaging to your welfare have been initiated. All tragedies can be revealed as blessings in disguise to those who are ready to open their eyes and recognize them as pointers to greater understanding of the true goal of their life.

So try to relinquish this fixed idea held by so many people who have never gone beyond Old Testament conceptions, that the often apparently unmerited diseases and disasters man experiences are forms of punishment. Far from it. Punishment is always an activity of humanity. Man seldom catches more than partial glimpses in the teachings of the Scriptures and his own observations of the true interpretation of all cosmic laws.

Another instance of this lack of understanding is the facile explanation of the Law of Causation as the "eye for an eye and a tooth for a tooth" theory held by so many in the West; this is both unenlightened and false, the result of purely human concepts of primitive justice and a materialistic way of thinking. It is always unwise to be too readily satisfied by such easy and superficial theories; they may be shadows of truth but more often distortions of it.

As I have tried to make you realize so often, man's ills are nearly always due to his own actions or to decisions taken in the higher and wiser aspect of his own being. They are the Soul's effort to purify and liberate his lower consciousness from all that is static and holds him in a state of crystallization or causes him to break divine law through ignorance. Only personality experience and the pressure upon him from his higher Self can help him achieve such freedom.

This brings us back again to the basic teaching that in order to become a *complete* human being all conditions of human experience have, at some time, to be absorbed, known "on the pulses", before eventually they can become qualities, powers, the intuitive capacity to identify with others in their struggles, ideals and joys. This is what development really means.

At the beginning of what is, in fact, a spiritual voyage of discovery into the self and the Self, it is of vital importance to keep on recalling the fact that so long as you deliberately misuse gifts, reject opportunities, are motivated by all those feelings and attitudes which are essentially separative, it will be you, at the higher level of your Soul who, in obedience to the Law of equilibrium, will *choose* sooner or later to evoke into a personal existence the opportunities by means of which restitution can be made and restoration of balance be achieved. I know that this has been emphasized again and again in these talks, but it is something which the mind so often conveniently forgets particularly when a realization of the implications of what most people would consider to be quite ordinary and reasonable behaviour might be too disturbing to peace of mind.

If a genuine attempt is to be made to clear the way of everything which still prevents further advance towards a condition of health and wholeness of being, many human joys for which you crave together with the opportunities which you feel you need in order to develop your natural gifts and capacities may well have been deliberately withheld in this life in order that other lines of development should be followed and other qualities still lacking be developed. This, and the payment of ancient debts, is of paramount importance from the point of view of the Soul.

You see again how unwise it is to draw any definite conclusions regarding the probable cause of events in any one specific life since the whole complex pattern cannot be perceived until you are in a far more advanced stage of development.

Knowledge of all the causes of present conditions would serve no real purpose except to confuse you. It is living *now* that is important, learning to accept and to deal with events as they come in the light of the understanding you have acquired. It is enough to recognize that what comes to each individual is never fortuitous but is due to what he has drawn to himself.

So if you desire a better and fuller life in the future you should start creating it in the present by developing all your potentialities and capacities to the best of your ability. But above all by increasing the ability to love and serve *where you now stand*.

The implications of this Law of causation which maintains the overall balance in the cosmos, the divine harmony of being, will become increasingly clear to you as you seek to enlarge your spiritual vision.

What is too often overlooked is that the conditions men call good, such as material benefits and even perfect health, can only become genuinely good if they are rightly used and enable their possessor to redistribute the powers and capacities they have brought him. If these are restricted in order to benefit the individual alone they can become a curse by thrusting him deeper into the mire of ignorance and materialism.

The parable of the rich young man in the Gospels illustrates this, as does that of the talents. These stand for gifts and powers loaned by the master of the vineyard (the Soul) to his servants. As I have pointed out in another connection the man who buried his talent was deprived of it or, more accurately, deprived himself of it since, by neglecting it, it was automatically "taken from him". Which means that as he had not used it to fulfil his life's purpose it became atrophied. Whereas those who did their best with what they had, increased their own capacities and were thereby fitted to receive more power and responsibility.

Deeper implications related to universal laws can always be found in the parables of Jesus by those who seek to discover their spiritual interpretations.

Never lose sight of the fact that man is on earth to grow—to become more than he now is by using every opportunity good or ill that life presents to him; for to *become* in the spiritual meaning of the word is to express in however small and restricted a way that Everbecoming aspect of Divinity—God Immanent.

Keeping all this in mind you will begin to see that while your hopes and dreams may not necessarily be realized in the forms in which they now exist, they can and will slowly change their nature into new forms more possible of fulfilment. This means that they will become transmuted in such a way that frustrations and trials on the physical plane will to a large extent lose their paramount importance to you.

There is a saying to the effect that: *If you cannot have what you want, it is better to learn to want what you have.* It is a crude and rather unconvincing way of expressing a real truth. For what you possess, what everyone, however humble and disregarded really possesses, is the potentially creative and redemptive light of the divine Self *within the personality*. Want this—desire it with your whole heart, and it will begin to stir and to transilluminate your world. So hold on to this source of super-material radiance and joy through the most menacing and dark phases of your life. Call upon it with conviction and it will lead you out of the valley of the shadow.

Do not give heed to all those who sneer and say that these ideas are just rationalizations, escapes from "reality". Ask them what they mean by "reality".

The greatest teachers the world has known never tire of emphasizing that Reality is to be sought in the inner significance of things and events rather than in the restricted forms by means of which truth can only as yet communicate itself to man in terms of his own limitations.

The apprehension of Reality rather than the many ephemeral goals to which ignorance more often than not points the way is the goal of all man's endeavour.

Analyse these lesser goals if you do not believe me. What for instance is the real nature of that yearning for possessions, for love or success, for fulfilment and happiness which drive mankind—as it has driven you—from experiment to experiment and so often from failure to failure and which never seems to be satisfied even by those who have attained their desires? Can you not see that such cravings, even though they may serve a useful purpose in spurring man to efforts he might not otherwise trouble to make and to experiences he would otherwise miss, are by no means fundamentally what they seem to be? They are nearly always man's false interpretation of urges emanating from far deeper levels, from the drive of the Soul, luring its personality like a will-o'-the wisp from experience to experience, or an endless search which forces him eventually to struggle out of the bog of illusion to more secure ground. For you tend to forget, as I pointed out to you earlier, that all these ideals, hopes, wishes, ambitions and dreams are symbols, in the final count, of their high spiritual counterparts or archetypes. They represent an unrecognized longing or the part for ultimate perfection—union with the divine Whole.

This is why many faiths stress the idea that man lives in a world of illusion.

Manifestation, experience, the perpetual tension between the pairs of opposites are real enough. They are of vital importance in all processes of growth. But it is the highly exaggerated measure of importance man gives to purely material achievements and satisfactions which is illusory because it is mistaking the symbol for the Reality.

All those who have spent many lives experimenting and exploring, wandering down side roads and in the labyrinths of ignorance, stress again and again that nothing less than realization of the nature of the inner divine unity of Life can give lasting satisfaction and that the way to achieve it is by a ceaseless effort to call into action the power of the Soul which works always for the ultimate good, not only of the individual, but of society.

XI

You are still inclined to waste far too much time, as indeed most people do, in daydreams and vague desires for a change in conditions, but even more often by going back into the past indulging either in longings or in vain regrets.

All this is futile unless it enables you to see your mistakes more clearly and use these memories to teach you the way in which cause and effect has worked out in your life.

But generally speaking such activities—if they can be so called, for they are essentially negative and static—are forms of escapism because the individual cannot face adequately the pressures, difficulties and responsibilities of the present.

There are many unrecognized dangers in this kind of self-indulgence for, improbable though it may seem to you, every regret, every reiterated conversation, every self-justification, as well as every yearning for a repetition of lost joys is inflicting injury upon yourself.

Not only is it charging you with negative and unproductive elements which can actually engender harmful physical and psychological reactions, but it is also a waste of time and energy which could be far better employed by acting creatively in the present instead of deliberately damming up forces which should be freed and directed to flow into future activities.

Also by dwelling upon what is past and therefore cannot be altered, you are acting like a squirrel in a cage busy going nowhere and never escaping from its bitter captivity. Think about this last word, for it is a very apt one.

There is another harmful effect such attitudes can have

particularly upon people like yourself. Because your past has been so full of frustrations and sorrows it inclines you to feel that there can be no hope of better things in the future. This pessimistic clinging to the pattern of the past tends to bring to pass the very situations you fear.

A real change can only be wrought in your life if you are prepared to make a supreme effort to move forward out of the old rhythms into a new approach to living.

Change is a law of nature. This I have often tried to impress upon you. Not to move on, therefore, at some level or another of the personality is to stagnate. This can also lead to various forms of disease, even to atrophy, cause and effect working here and now in the present life.

Man possesses, within certain limitations, choice and free will; so by deliberately choosing to bury himself in the grave of the past he is breaking another divine law, that of evolution, of progression from one stage to the next and is bound to suffer the consequences.

What I want to make clear to you is that if, in the future, loss, sorrow or disaster should come to you there is no need to take it for granted that they must affect you in the same way as they have done hitherto. For, if you have made the effort to change your normal reactions, acquired what I must call a different "receiving apparatus" you will thereby have become to some extent a *different person*. You will be armed with new insights and new powers of resistance.

In the past many of your reactions have arisen largely from lack of understanding of the meaning and purpose of life; the inability to accept that every experience has in it the potentiality of an advance in growth, a new phase in development.

Filled with resentment and despair you have often deliberately rejected experience, shut your eyes to the opportunities it offered you. In thus refusing to let yourself be swept forward into the future you have at the same time refused those gifts, powers and insights awaiting you there, and by thus damming up the natural movement of the Life force you have yourself been instrumental in causing those forms of sickness which are directly due to this kind of negation of life.

For no benefits can come to you, no new insights, no light infinitely higher than the personality levels if you deliberately block them by such attitudes.

Examine yourself. Why do you react in this way? May there not be in you an as yet unrecognized desire for martyrdom, a secret wish to be an object of pity and concern behind this emphasis you have always put upon your misfortunes?

You see, we are always returning to the admonition: *Man know thyself*. Without self-knowledge man is always the victim of his self-deceptions.

What I have said today applies, of course, not only to you but to everyone, young and old.

The young, more especially, are making their future here on earth by all they think and do; they are creating themselves anew all the while with the malleable material of youth which has not yet taken on those many fixed ideas and standpoints, those dogmas about life which so hamper growth. So they have infinite and glorious opportunities if only they can learn in time what life is for.

But even for the old, who have passed beyond the possibility of many creative experiments with life, there can still be compensations and inner satisfactions, the fruits which should normally develop from the blossoms of wisely assimilated experience. So growth can continue until the end of life here making them a source of help and love to those around them.

The old have also a future for which they can and should prepare—that next stage of their life journey awaiting them beyond the frontiers of death which is but a continuation or an extension of their present life-consciousness. It is important that everyone, even the young, should realize that their condition after death will correspond to that state which characterized them on earth. There are no real breaks, the flow of life goes on eternally.

So be wise and equip yourself now for this journey, feeding heart and mind on all wise and lovely things so that you may enter this new phase prepared for what may there be disclosed to you.

Unfortunately for them, very few ageing people do this. Most prefer, as you have done hitherto, to look backwards and in consequence spend their last years eating the rinds and husks of vain regrets.

Even as the springs of water well up from below the earth, so the living waters should be sought below the surface of appearances.

I would emphasize once more that just as your reaction to past events has made you what you now are, so your reaction to the present is already influencing and forming the future in the after-life and in earth lives beyond that. Thus the wheel of what men think of as Destiny turns. But you have power to a greater extent than you believe to control that wheel yourself once you learn to meet events by the new creative methods I have tried to show you.

So make up your mind to begin now—at once—to deal with everything that happens to you in this new way.

Thought and desire, as I have so often stressed, possess dynamic power for inaugurating change, particularly when they are allied to imagination. This knowledge is of very special importance to all those who tend to be negative and who easily despair.

Is this not proved by history? Has not every radical change for the better first existed as a thought in one man's mind conceived by an enlightened imagination?

Even the forces of nature bow before the creative energy of man's thoughts because matter is essentially the servant of mind.

Man is all the while despatching his thoughts and desires to the furthest confines not alone of his own kingdom but far beyond. Like messengers good or evil, beneficial or destructive, they are perpetually at work affecting him and his world in innumerable subtle and unrecognized ways. If not in this incarnation then in future ones humanity cannot escape their results.

Given sufficient knowledge and power man could even make of his body what he chose, revitalizing it by means of thought. But of course in order to do this he would have had to have freed himself from all the Karma of his past.

It is said that the great saints or adepts, the true illuminati, do possess such powers. Did Jesus, perhaps, use such knowledge when his body was placed in the tomb, disintegrating the physical atoms and reintegrating them when he wished to show himself to his followers? Aspects of this arcane knowledge were sought by the alchemists, although the majority did not realize that it was a spiritual rather than a material elixir they would have to discover.

With this in mind you should be able to see more clearly now why I have tried to impress upon you that thoughts of envy, hate, jealousy, resentment and indifference to the troubles of one's fellow men are so especially dangerous to health and happiness. Remember that it is their power to build up toxic areas in the *total* organism which extends, of course, far beyond the physical body, that is so pernicious because it is the subtle atoms that will be used to construct the various bodies in the future. These will inevitably be, in consequence, infected by such poisons.

What is almost, if not quite as important, is the fact

that since you, at every level, are an intrinsic part of the body of humanity, by thus infecting yourself you are also helping to infect this greater body; and the harm you do to it you must obviously be doing also to yourself. A vicious circle until you break it with deliberate intent. I have stressed this often in many ways too but repeat it again because it is of such vital importance that you realize how great the responsibility of every single individual is.

Seek, therefore, to cleanse yourself from all destructive tendencies so that you may begin to radiate positive, curative energies which will lead to greater health, wholeness and happiness.

There is no need to despair if your attempts still seem feeble and unconstructive. No effort you make can fail to affect, in however small a degree, the climate of your environment and consequently far wider fields since all are intrinsically one with you and there is no real break in the total warp and weft of Life.

This was the inner meaning of the words of Jesus: "Inasmuch as ye have done it to the least of these little ones, ye have done it unto me." For he was the prototype of universal man made perfect.

Nor was it only of the children of the earth of whom he spoke, but of every weaker and smaller organism, even down to cellular life, which it is humanity's task to direct, aid and purify by the way he lives and thinks so as to bring all things ultimately towards perfection.

XII

As you have at last really accepted the basic proposition that the present existence is only a phase in a process of spiritual unfoldment, one aspect of that stream of experience which comprises many previous essays in living in the material world, you should have realized that each separate experience is a signpost, essential during one particular stage of the journey in order to point the way to the next.

Once, however, any stage has been attained and passed and its lessons absorbed, it should be related to that specific moment in development and to the particular lessons or problems with which the traveller had to deal. If he cannot say honestly that he has learned everything it was designed to teach him, he must accept the fact that he is not yet ready to take the next step upon his way.

Now you have found that again and again similar signposts have reappeared, similar sets of circumstances, similar problems have repeated themselves. So you would be wise to recognize when they do that this is an indication that you have not yet thoroughly explored them nor read the message they were designed to convey. This really means that you have not discovered in yourself the reasons which reactivated them in your life-pattern.

Because of this reiteration you often suffer from despair as might a traveller who, thinking that his road leads straight on, finds instead that it curves backwards bringing him again to his starting-place.

But I would reassure you. This is not time wasted. Something has been learned even though the traveller may not yet be consciously aware of it. What you should do is to make a special effort to discover the reason for this recurrence, for until you succeed in doing so you will be faced again and again with a similar situation.

So do not wonder and do not complain. Set to work to solve the riddle. Accept it as a message which must be decoded. Study it in depth to see in what particular way or at what level one situation resembles the other and where you have failed in dealing with it. In order to be successful you must try to remain as detached as possible. There must be no self-pity, no gloss of sentimentality, no search for excuses to absolve you from failure. Use your knowledge of psychology as well as plain commonsense, but above all the deeper understanding you should by now have acquired to enable your eyes to be opened.

As you work at resolving such problems you will realize increasingly that each time you have missed the heart of the matter owing to your own blindness and ignorance. What may have led you back to the same milestone could be some unresolved complex in your character, faulty judgment or possibly just lack of love resulting in failure to try to perfect a relationship which, again and again in the past has set a similar chain of effects in motion.

For make no mistake; the present only repeats the pattern of the past in this life or another when the development has been arrested at some given point, so that work which should have been accomplished has been left unfinished. Thus the law of cause and effect work in with the will of the Soul to perfect its instrument. Over and over again the attempt will be made to lead the personality to acquire those specific qualities needed for the immediate task.

As I have emphasized many times you should learn to look upon the past, whatever its nature, only as your teacher and your failures as guides, leading you to understand more of your own weakness and spiritual needs. Once any specific lesson has been learned then the only value in dwelling on the past is in using your experiences to help others in similar situations.

A warning here. In order to do this effectively it is important to watch yourself with special care and to avoid letting personal reactions influence the advice you give. However, if you make yourself increasingly sensitive to your inner voice you can be guided to approach those you wish to help in the right way; for this needs much wisdom. You must remember never to thrust what you consider to be truth at anyone in a dogmatic and too positive manner. There are as many paths to wisdom in one sense as there are individuals; in fact it has been said that: "each man is unto himself the way". Discover through sympathetic identification the sufferer's specific path, then help him to find truth upon it, but never try to force him on to your path. When you feel he may be ready to seek one other than his own, then offer him what you believe you have to give.

Proselytizing does more harm than good. One must not try to break down barriers, but armed with wisdom and love one can often transform them into open gates leading to a wider, lighter landscape.

I tell you this because you must learn to give what you have received to others in need, but it is always *how* to give which confuses the well-intentioned novice.

One of the main hindrances to the development of greater receptivity and openness to truth is to be tied to preconceived ideas and unthinking acceptance of childish interpretations of those symbols by means of which truth has been presented in other ages when man was less mentally developed than he is today. Only too often these become shackles about the feet of seekers after Reality.

It should be realized by all those who cling to the dogmas of any religion that basic Reality cannot be presented to the average mind in any but symbolical form.

As man's perceptions develop so these symbols must change. In consequence those who cling tenaciously to past interpretations of the eternal truths are attuning themselves to a stream of energies which have almost lost their living quality and are gradually acquiring a condition analogous to hardening of the arteries. Many religions today are suffering this fate and many diseases are also the result of a sick person clinging tenaciously to concepts and attitudes which, animated by currents of energy now in their decline, should be relinquished.

Fluidity, a readiness to change, to adapt to new situations and ideas, seeking always what changes indicate from a deeper point of view—their more universal, spiritual significance—is a prerequisite to growth and to health.

This tendency to cling to the past is, as you know yourself, one of the causes of your many difficulties. Sometimes you still appear to me as one encased in a veritable chrysalis of fixed ideas. The more you allow these to dominate you, the more difficult it will be to free yourself from them. Material which is petrified, obdurate, set in a hard mould, must perforce be shaped anew by sharp blows. For the chrysalis must be broken before the butterfly (symbol of the Soul) can emerge. How can you spread translucent wings to the sun while they remain pressed to your sides by the restricting bonds of outworn shibboleths, of superstitions, stultifying fears and, worst of all, an identification with the kind of personality you have been all your life, but need be no more?

Now, at last, you can begin to free yourself. The whole of the teachings I have given you are to help release you and all m like case from this form of imprisonment. It is man's fatal illusions about life and its true meaning which prevent him from opening himself out to the forces of liberation and renewal.

Let your illusions go. The time for you to begin to live

more positively, more realistically, more optimistically is *now*.

I assure you, as I have done so often before, that you will gain strength and encouragement from every genuine effort you make, for each will help you to align yourself more closely to the universal Source of all strength and power.

Strengthened by these forces of spiritual health you will become capable of shaping the stones of the present into the shining temple of the future.

I know that you still find this difficult to believe, but this is only because at moments you are obsessed by fears of what the future holds to such an extent that you cannot shake yourself free and, even after all we have discussed together, continue wasting much time and energy in attempting to penetrate the veil which hides it in search of reassurance. But why can you not see that the future is always in process of being created out of every daily thought, action and decision?

It is in this ability to reshape and renew himself and consequently his own destiny that man's greatest opportunity and also his hope lie. I am always trying to impress this upon you because if you truly desire to break out of the old chrysalis you must cease to dwell upon that imperfect image of yourself you have built up by reason of your past inadequacy, weakness and failures. You—the personality—can henceforth be guided, if you will, by this centre of power which dwells within you and is capable of transforming all these negative forces which still dominate you into positive powers of health and regeneration.

The present is yours; use it. It is the womb in which your future is conceived.

So affirm unwaveringly that the future is truly yours to make and build. You alone, charged with these life-giving energies of the Soul can fashion it in an infinitely finer shape than ever before, a thing of beauty and worth.

Inasmuch as your present qualities and capacities are the direct result of the efforts you have made in the past, does it not follow that if you so choose you may nourish the seeds still latent within you so that they may flower in the future into greater and more beneficent powers than you have ever known?

Cease then, from this very moment, to be like so many of your contemporaries who ignorantly persist in identifying themselves only with the dense material substance of matter and in consequence are totally conditioned by the turmoil and conflicts which constitute the normal activities of humanity. These will always hold man prisoner until he gains spiritual insight into their significance and learns to identify them with the unbalanced forces in his own nature. Only then will he discover how peace on earth can be attained.

You have been imprisoned by them in too many lives and for too many years in the present one. But you have now arrived at a point when you can free yourself.

It cannot be done by one supreme effort, but by a hundred delicate threads, created like the spider out of yourself, all day and every day in every kind of situation. These are the strands which at last will become a bridge linking you, whenever you attempt to cross it in thought with your true Self, until at last you can cross it freely and enter into a state of greater light and wisdom than you have ever known.

Then, and then only, will you realize the purpose of the harsh discipline of pain and frustration you have experienced in this life and be thankful that you have had to undergo it.

XIII

Do not let yourself be so depressed by your recurrent moods of despair at your slow rate of progress and angry with yourself because you are so seldom able to practise with success the exercises I have suggested to you.

I know that at times it seems to you that the very efforts you are making precipitate upon you more acute sufferings and more severe trials; you feel that for every step you advance you are forced back two; that the valley grows darker the further it is penetrated and at each height surmounted, each corner turned, greater heights appear and the path you travel is revealed as winding on endlessly before your weary eyes.

But in many ways this is a good sign. It indicates movement and the growth of greater realization. If you had not made progress you would not be able to perceive these new, even if alarming, vistas. This increased awareness of what must still be done is, therefore, reason for hope rather than despair. You have learned much of which you have hitherto been ignorant; not only the true causes of so many of your troubles, but infinitely more valuable, that it is possible in any situation to invoke guidance and strength from your own Soul and even from those who watch humanity from higher levels with deep love and understanding and always respond to a genuine cry for help.

Because you have reached a stage where you have become more conscious than ever before of your own weaknesses and needs, setbacks take on a more serious aspect. But this is a stage only, however long and dark it may seem to you. If you continue to press on it must be left behind. The darkest valley has an end.

Remember, light dissipates darkness, and even here and now light is all about you at all times even when you are least aware of it. By turning your attention away from the difficulties and failures whenever you can and invoking this all-embracing light it will illuminate the path ahead of you as you walk on.

As we have seen in earlier talks the deliberate fixing of attention upon any specific aspect of life will draw you to it and it to you. Hence the importance of concentrating only upon the good, the true and the beautiful, these forces which make for harmony and health.

This applies of course to every form of activity, physical, mental as well as spiritual. *There is but one Life and one Law*.

Consider once again the athlete. A man who decides to train for any kind of sport has to undergo a long and strenuous discipline. He does not become a boxer or a runner in a few weeks. If he has not been in training for a number of years, even though he may have considered himself to be strong and healthy, the moment he begins to exercise his unaccustomed muscles he will suffer severe aches and pains. But if he is determined to reach his goal he will accept these temporary discomforts, these physical strains and stresses, and be prepared to make every sacrifice necessary: sacrifices of diet, of pleasure, of time. In fact his whole life will have to be readjusted and tuned in, as it were, to his purpose.

If the athlete who, after all, is only training for the most ephemeral of ends and striving after a comparatively insignificant prize, is prepared to undergo such discipline and to make such serious and prolonged efforts, what must be expected of him whose objective is an eternal and supernal one, the prize for which will be greater fulfilment, greater bliss than the human mind can conceive?

Remember the effort must always be commensurate with the goal.

If you truly desire to be healed at *every* level, redeemed and freed from the effects of spiritual blindness, discipline and unshakable resolution, the ability to pick yourself up each time you stumble and fall is essential.

What is more, the instrument must be tempered for its use. This is bound to take time. Just as no stable edifice can be built upon the decaying ruins of the old, so first there is much basic work to be done on the foundations before one can begin to build a new and more noble temple which, in order to endure, must be raised on a firmer structure.

Therefore you must take into account the conditions in which you now have to work. Since you have never attempted seriously to deal with your normal reactions to failure in the past, how can you expect to succeed at once in this attempt which is virtually to reverse your whole life-pattern?

When the body has been neglected or weakened by any form of excess, the greater must be the time and effort which will have to be spent upon the preliminary period of preparation and training, and the more violent will be the reactions of the unbalanced part of the economy. And unfortunately so far as you are concerned in this and many lives you have neglected the spiritual aspects of your being and weakened the resistance of your emotional and physical forces by concentration upon your personal desires at the expense of others. There is much in consequence to be faced and endured, and you will need great patience, which is particularly difficult for you with your ambition and characteristic eagerness to succeed in all you undertake.

But I have warned you before that to demand too much of oneself in the beginning, to rush towards the goal instead of consolidating each step, is particularly dangerous in an endeavour such as this. Impatience for results could mean that your hidden motives are question-

able and are due, perhaps, to a subtle form of vanity or
pride. Think about what I have said. It is a factor of
major importance that motives must be as pure and
untainted by personal weakness as possible, for the attempt
upon which you have now willingly embarked is the most
important step man can take; it is the turning-point in the
whole long series of lives which lead from earth to heaven;
therefore it is essential to develop an objective and
balanced attitude at the outset.

This, the incarnating Self, which shaped for its purpose
the personality with which hitherto you have been almost
wholly identified, is now attempting to achieve. But its
task is particularly hard owing to the material brought
over from the past. These handicaps your early experiences (again, remember, the results of inner choice)
accentuated owing to the ignorance of parents and
teachers and your own foolishness, as you well know. In
view of this and of the fact that it is only recently that
you have begun the attempt to listen to the inner voice of
your Soul, it is inevitable that the negative forces should
still be so powerful. How can you reasonably hope to correct immediately all those erroneous habits of thought
and action which have evolved through the years of the
present life and indeed long before that? It would never be
expected, much less demanded of you.

But the more you succeed in holding firmly to the
knowledge you have already gained regarding the nature
of your true Self the more surely the sense of your intrinsic
unity with it will grow until it becomes a permanent
reality.

So in those dark hours you dread when the imprisoned
self rebels, turning away from all theories and beliefs and
stubbornly declares: "I am alone; I am weak and helpless;
I am nothing," when there is neither will to good nor
even desire for it, when the weary body rejects the Soul,
its master, turning all sweetness sour by feeding itself

upon every poison of bitterness and hate which remains
untransmuted in the deeper levels of self; when even
loved faces become masks; when in despair you cry aloud:
"Who shall deliver me from the body of this death?"
make a supreme effort to recall all you have been told and
to realize that this is a part of the process of transmutation
leading to release from the darkness in which you are
plunged.

It is just at these lowest and weakest moments that the
most powerful affirmations of unity with the Higher
should be made. For the very effort to do this strikes the
note to which the Soul always responds. Although
nothing may seem to happen immediately and the darkness remains impenetrable, the note does not cease to
vibrate or have an effect and as soon as this vibration
grows strong enough light will break through to dissipate
the shadows which are confusing and stupefying the
lower consciousness.

Ask yourself at such times of doubt: "Is truth less truth
when it becomes entangled in a net of doubts? Is the sun
less bright because the clouds have veiled it from our
sight?" Not so. Nor are you any less your true and
glorious Self because there has been a severence of contact caused by long years of ignorance and your own present lack of power and knowledge to control or to rise
above the dark mists of the lower realms.

Remember, you and your Soul are working together
now as the unity (which in fact you are) in this project
of developing permanent conscious co-operation. You
are both building the bridge which will span the illusory
gulf between what is, in truth, but *one being*.

Has it not occurred to you that occasionally you might
be deliberately cut off here in order to stimulate you into
making a supreme effort to reach up to higher levels?
By no means always, of course. There are plenty of other
causes which could bring about one of these sudden

descents into apparent isolation which cause you such despair.

However cut off you may feel yourself to be, it will help if you try to recall those flashes of realization which have come to you from the realms of Reality during these treatments. For once they have been experienced in the lower consciousness they can never again be wholly lost. They remain a permanent possession and are not beyond recall. They are glimpses of what is in essence your eternal heritage.

But you have concentrated so long upon the objective aspects of life that numinous and subjective states are all the more difficult to attain. Since they operate in subtle matter, you will inevitably find that it will take time before you become consciously aware of them. But I can assure you that this will change as you meditate more upon these greater realities still hidden by the dense material world. Each attempt you make to work in with the will of the Soul, every time you deliberately replace a negative or destructive thought by a positive and more enlightened one of creative love and harmony adds, as it were, another small brick which, conforming more closely to the grand design of the Architect, advances the rebuilding of the total structure which is yourself to a finer and nobler pattern.

Only when this new edifice has advanced beyond the dimensions of the old will you be enabled to perceive its outlines more clearly and become conscious of its beauty and enduring strength. Then at last you will begin to feel increasingly secure and aware of what has been happening during the long struggles and within the darkness which now seems so often impenetrable and changeless. No longer will you be so afraid of the dust caused by falling debris, the noise of hammers and of drills which are a necessary phase in any reconstruction.

At the moment you will have to accept these stages

more or less blindly; but you should remind yourself that however many times you still feel overcome by a sense of inadequacy and failure the building goes on.

Let me impress upon you yet again what I have emphasized from the beginning of these treatments.

Try, when you find yourself threatened by despair and a sense of struggling against insuperable odds to keep in mind the concept of yourself as a small cell in a greater Life, one with God's will and purpose. The clearer you can see yourself thus, the more surely you will be drawn into an ever greater consciousness of and participation in the purpose of man's creation—to bring all beings at last to know themselves one in That which is all love, all power, all bliss. Why need you, then, fear or despair? You are on your way.

XIV

THERE is an even profounder significance to suffering of which I have not yet spoken, but I believe you are now more ready to consider the general idea even if you cannot hope to grasp its deeper implications, for I can only touch the surface of such a profoundly esoteric subject.

Let us again turn to the basic concept of the absolute unity of Life. We have often considered the role of the cells within any single structure and the fact that if one cell ceases to play its allotted part and "runs wild" the effect it would have on the whole, by setting up a chain reaction, could be disastrous. Analogously, since all living things are, in a wider connotation, cells in greater bodies or centres of life each must have an influence upon its own specific group in accordance with its specific reactions to experience.

So far as man is concerned his groups consist of his family unit, and those with whom he is affiliated most closely throughout his life, in his work, social contacts and above all by affinity. Therefore his behaviour and beliefs must, to some extent, influence them all.

But what is not generally realized is that the Soul is also itself affiliated with wider groups at its own level. This can include groups both in and out of incarnation.

On earth the members of a group may not necessarily feel very close to each other or at least may not hold together for any great length of time; but soul groups have been built up through collaboration and close affinity in many past relationships both in and out of incarnation, and consequently endure infinitely longer owing to these and other causes of an even more deeply esoteric nature.

Each Soul group is linked with others at higher levels, just as groups are on earth, and this complex extends upward and onward throughout the universe even to the planes of the great angels and probably beyond.

Try, for a moment, to imagine this intricate network, myriads of centres of intelligent life, each influencing each by means of its specific radiation, each playing its part in the total divine plan.

In a somewhat similar way, of course, an earth group, engaged on some specific project, can radiate an influence beyond its own network to all who are on a similar wavelength and respond to its note, although its members may never have met each other in the flesh.

In this age group influence is increasing as never before owing to the many new forms of communication. Newspapers, radio and above all television bring the problems and disasters of the world into each individual's life. In consequence the power which strong emotions or strongly directed thought can exercise upon the total human situation is immeasurable.

As we have seen earlier, power is generated by close interest and by attention, both of which are part of the techniques employed by those whose work is communication. The result is to strengthen the subtle links between groups and any who may be receptive and open to thought-transference and other extrasensory influences. The sensitive are particularly vulnerable and such methods of transmission should only be utilized by those who desire to help their fellow men in a generalized way, but pressure should never be put upon others, even in what may be considered by the transmitter to be a "good" cause.

But there are many special invocations and prayers which can be very effective when used legitimately in this way to direct currents of healing, love and spiritual strength to those in need.

Thus you should now be able to realize to what an

extent experiences, however personal they may seem to the individual, contribute to the total sum of the experiences of this aggregate of lives—this world group of humanity which, for want of a better term could be called the "world-being". It is the synthesis of this close inner as well as outer participation which helps to create what is recognized as the "climate" of an age.

Each separate unit of this world group, besides working out his own individual Karma is also inescapably involved in the specific Karma of his own group, his nation, his race and the conditions obtaining in the *whole*—which must also include the natural world—for he is an integral part of it. One can see an indication of this operating in collective disasters such as earthquakes and nations seized by the madness of war.

There are many far deeper implications in this teaching of group participation in suffering which you may discover when you meditate upon the whole question.

No one can escape from this involvement and the responsibility it imposes upon every unit in this vast network to contribute to it nothing but what is good, constructive and empowered by love.

Even if a man believes he can hold himself apart in an attitude of neutrality and non-commitment, he is breaking the divine law of right-relationship by depriving others of what he might contribute; in consequence he will have to make good this act in one life or another. By the very act of living one is incurring obligations at every level since everything man does or refrains from doing is affecting the conditions in his world in dense or subtle matter, not only by what his actions contribute but also by the subtle emission of magnetic currents, negative or positive, destructive or creative, good or evil, which telepathically convey impulses or messages throughout the entire network.

These can naturally take many forms. For instance on

F

the mental level they would consist mainly of ideas or concepts which others on a similar wavelength could pick up and adopt thinking them to be their own. But it is at the emotional level that such waves are more potent and more dangerous because so many more people are predominantly emotionally polarized.

You see now how vitally important it is to watch your thoughts and emotional discharges?

Because time and space have no meaning so far as the transference of thought or powerfully energized emotions are concerned, people on similar wavelengths can be influenced throughout the world very easily for good or ill.

So when your moods are dark, resentful, filled with self-pity and over-concern with your own troubles you may be infecting like a virus people quite unknown to you who are in a state of receptivity, suffering themselves perhaps from deep depression or on the edge of despair. Power-fully charged emotions such as those of hatred or violence are even more infectious and can intensify attitudes which may be as yet only nascent or potential in another person attuned to them.

The extent of the responsibility of each individual for the atmosphere not only around him but equally for that of his times cannot be exaggerated nor recalled to mind too often.

Incidentally it is salutary to keep reminding yourself that the kind of force you emanate will inevitably affect you also. There is no possibility of evading such conse-quences since no action or thought of sufficient intensity to register on the surrounding atmosphere is without some influence on the individual who produces it.

There is of course the other side of the picture to consider. It should encourage you and all those who are seeking to aid humanity at this critical time to realize how powerful your thoughts and your every response to need can be for good. By assiduously cultivating awareness of the needs of others, goodwill, warmth in your relationships, love and joyous acceptance of every experience as a means to a divine end, you will be, quite literally helping to enlighten the atmosphere not only about you personally, but in far wider spheres, for you may be transmitting telepathically strength and courage to those you may never meet but who are still bound together with you in this subtle and invisible network of human lives.

This effort is of particular importance at the present time because so many are in acute physical, emotional and mental distress owing, as I have already told you, to the enormous stresses under which humanity as a whole is labouring and the widespread awareness of mass suffering on the planet. It would help to alleviate this agony to some extent at least if there was a better understanding of the reasons for the situation, but more especially the part unavoidable suffering can—and indeed does—play in arousing man from apathy and inspiring the desire to help and to serve; in fact it stimulates the forces of love and idealism in many in whom they have remained dormant hitherto. It can also give the individual a sense of proportion so that his own misfortunes become more bearable and appear less arbitrary.

But there is even more to it than this.

One striking example of the influence personal suffering can have on a world-wide scale we have already discussed, but you have not entirely realized its full implications as it relates to what I have called world-karma. This is when those who, having been afflicted by some specific form of disability, not only rise above it but devote their lives to the attempt to alleviate the lot of their fellow sufferers either through their own experiments or by example in proving, by the manner in which they overcome the handicap, that it is still possible to live a good and useful life.

Think, too, of the enormous advances which have been made in medical knowledge through the treatment of wounds caused by war and accident and by intensive research in a more general attempt to cure endemic disease.

Thus world imbalance or what has been called "collective Karma" can be to some extent adjusted and also mitigated by the sufferings and sacrifices of the few. Here I am touching upon another very deep mystery of which even the great sages admit to knowing little and which I can only leave to your intuition.

In this tremendous world-wide effort to deal with disease you have an example of the dictum that action and reaction are equal and opposite; intense darkness always calls forth a compensatory effort to increase light. You are faced now with another example in your world. Man's natural destructiveness of his environment through self-interest is beginning to open his eyes to his dependence upon the natural world and the realization that this too is an integral part of himself. This is forcing him to start protecting and preserving it if only for the sake of his own survival.

Those who are striving, as you are now doing, to gain greater insight into and understanding of the deeper significance of all that happens to themselves and their world, should never be content with facile and obvious explanations of any phenomena, particularly regarding the emotional realms where forces are most strong and therefore most potentially dangerous.

There is another aspect of suffering of which I have spoken before, but could be repeated here with advantage. This is the theory that many sufferers could well have chosen deliberately before birth to accept the burden of sickness in order to pay some debt to the community or simply out of pure compassion. But there may be even deeper implications in acts such as this and other sacrifices made by the few for the many. I can only give you a hint but it may help you to get a more balanced attitude.

Might not the aim of such men perhaps be to help lift, if only temporarily, some of the weight of what might be called collective evil generated down the ages by humanity, which has become too great for mankind to deal with and transmute? May this not have been attempted before by many saints and saviours who, we are told, have voluntarily descended into the terrible restrictions of a physical body in order to teach people how to live more wisely and so save themselves from their self-made hells?

It is said that at each period of acute crisis—and man is certainly passing through one today—a number of highly evolved souls descend into the world voluntarily in order to help humanity survive the impact of the destructive forces it has itself evoked. Such men and women can be of many faiths or may care nothing in their earth consciousness about religion in any of its now degraded forms; but the true understanding of the divine laws are there, implanted in their hearts; they are born enveloped in the light of the Soul and it is Soul impulse which spurs them on to such sacrifices.

But there are yet still deeper implications in the general condition of sickness and evil in the world. Too deep at present for man's understanding, although it may help you to meditate upon it.

Is this condition not endemic? Did sickness and violence not exist here before the advent of man, but increased their hold on life on earth through his ignorance and lusts?

The more you consider such questions the more you will come to realize the profundity of the mysteries which exist behind appearances for which man at his present stage should not expect to receive cut and dried explanations on demand. If such were given him he could be sure they were not the right ones: for the unavoidable use of words and phrases which are of man's making cannot possibly express concepts relating to insights into truth he is not yet fitted to acquire.

But the few hints I have given you during these treatments should at least have enabled you to take in future a rather wider view of the massive troubles of mankind. And the more you meditate upon them the more you will begin to realize that no suffering can be utterly fortuitous or useless. Something can always be learned from it not only by the individual but, in some form or another, by that wider consciousness of the group of individuals I have called the "world being".

So try to see yourself increasingly as a vitally important unit in a world plan; an instrument created by your Soul not only to help in the transmutation of the destructive forces caused by your own previous errors, but also to participate in a far greater endeavour, in that *collective* attempt being made by a great proportion of mankind, blindly and instinctively for the most part so far as personalities are concerned, to transmute dross into gold.

I stress yet again that to the extent that your personal sufferings are bravely and cheerfully borne, so that no negative vibrations are any longer permitted to influence the atmosphere of your world, you can become even in this life a source of strength and blessing by uniting in thought with all those who are seeking to help humanity.

This is a high destiny. Recall it in your dark hours of pain or despair. You can become one with the flower of mankind in this common endeavour if you so will.

Realize at the same time that unlike the average man and woman who suffers blindly in ignorance of the purpose behind their condition, you are especially blessed because you have earned the right to greater understanding, and above all possess the possibility of uniting yourself with the redemptive forces of your Soul.

Make better use of your imagination. Try, during these moods of obscuration of the light which still so often possess you, to see yourself as a fragment of what is indeed in essence an angelic power. See it taking upon itself the burden of life in the form for the set purpose of attempting to cleanse one tiny part of the whole from the dark accretions which it has gathered round it down the ages. For you, and indeed every human being, are so immeasurably greater than the forms in which you are temporarily housed and by means of which you are inevitably diminished.

It is very important that this should be recognized and then kept in mind, as it will make a great difference to your attitude towards your suffering companions here. You are all diminished by immersion in these dense swathes of substance. Once this is realized it should make one of the worst aspects of separateness—criticism and condemnation—no longer possible. I have impressed it upon you several times before; but the elimination of such destructive activities is so important that I feel it necessary to emphasize it yet again and again.

Remind yourself, when you are about to criticize another that you can have no idea of his true spiritual status; he could be far more advanced than any of his critics but has been cut off from his true capacities in order that he shall concentrate upon dealing with certain problems hitherto avoided or forces he has been put on earth specifically to purify. Or he may have volunteered to come into the world with the express purpose of ministering to the "spirits in prison" by meeting them at their own level.

Only the higher Self can know the real reasons why its personality is as it is. It also knows to the last iota the personality's limitations and its potentialities. In view of this you may be sure that nothing is ever demanded of it, no burden is ever placed upon it which it has not the capacity to deal with once it learns to invoke the infinite power of that divinity of which it is an inseparable part.

Remember this, too, when you feel you are being strained beyond endurance and believe you have reached breaking-point. There are always spiritual reserves upon which you can call.

Read yet again the parable of the talents. Try to see yourself as a talent. It does not matter in what environment you are placed—or rather have been placed for this incarnation—whether it be humble or spectacular, in bad physical conditions or good ones, your conditions should be seen as a gift from a divine source which you, dweller-in-the-body, have been given to use as wisely and constructively as you can and must try to increase in value by means of knowledge, wisdom and the growing ability to radiate love into your environment.

So try to do each task, face every problem however trivial, as if it were of vital importance to the Whole. Then, slowly at first, yet inevitably you will come to realize more and more of those potentialities which exist behind the screen of your personality failures and weaknesses, but which until now have remained latent and unrecognized.

By thus gradually transcending your prison-house of form, by expanding your consciousness here through the power of your spirit until the imperfect and limited can contain it no more, you will be creating through the transforming energy of love a greater habitation, that true expression of your Soul wherein all aspects can dwell together in harmony.

Only then will a personality be born which will be enabled to radiate the joy that springs from the boundless Power which at last has found its focus—a soul-infused, love-conscious and God-conscious human being.

XV

THERE is one particular aspect of the Wisdom Teaching, upon which all spiritual healing is based, that you find impossible to understand much less to accept but which, nevertheless leaves you no peace.

This is hardly surprising as you are trying to solve with the mental faculties one of the greatest of the meta-physical mysteries. Nor do I pretend to be able to give you an explanation which could wholly satisfy the intellect. I have already told you the reason why this is impossible.

You ask: "What is this mystic union of which so many teachers speak when ultimately the dewdrop—the traveller through time—is lost in the Shining Ocean? Is this to be the end of all man's endeavours, his sufferings, his struggles, to lose all consciousness of himself, to lose indeed that very Self which he has been told to find? If all is ultimately to become One in total fusion, in a state of utter non-separativeness, where is the lover and where the beloved? How can the concept of love be apprehended apart from duality? Is a condition which can only be conceived of as annihilation be the end product of this inconceivable process through aeons of time which we call evolution?"

Such questions have been asked ever since man began his search for the ultimate truth about himself, his destiny and that of the universe. That they should be asked is right and good, for the spirit of man expands by means of ex-ploration into the unknown by stretching itself to the utter-most, by the ceaseless struggle to transcend its limitations.

At the same time it is absurd to torment yourself, as you still do. As I have said so often how could anything so imperfect and indeed embryonic as the intellect even begin to apprehend the mysteries of the purpose of the Perfect and the Illimitable?

Those members of various religious cults who claim to be able to give rational answers to such questions as you have put are suffering from a form of spiritual arrogance as great as that of those others who claim that because no material proof of the existence of God can be found, there can be no God. It is the truly wise man who is always ready to admit to his limitations.

To return to your difficulties. It is still possible, after accepting that ultimate truth is beyond the powers of any limited being to apprehend, that even greater degrees of reality can be attained by means of some of the techniques of meditation, by study, by asking questions of Life, by trying to decipher symbolical utterances of the sages, but most of all, perhaps, by aspiration. Those who have already developed qualities of inner vision and intuition can by these means arouse a movement in the depths of their being which sparks off a sudden flash of revelation, of penetrating spiritual insight. For it is taught that the One Life is focused *in its entirety* in its every aspect.

A meaningless phrase to the majority, but meditate upon it just the same.

You are confused by the saying that the dewdrop will be lost in the Ocean. What is this but a metaphor? It has also been said that eventually the Ocean fills the dewdrop. Transformation is not the same as annhilation. If the dewdrop should expand until it became the Ocean, or if the Ocean in some incomprehensible way, poured its total consciousness into that single atom of itself, would there not be for that atom infinite gain? All such metaphors present truth symbolically in terms of time, space and form, but Reality is beyond these. It has also been said: *Become what you* are, *then you will know.*

And as mental gymnastics will never arrive at resolving any problems relating to the concept of Reality or ultimate Truth, why despair? You have not yet even begun to develop those faculties by means of which alone man can soar with spiritual wings into the empyrean and be carried to realms of which few have ever had the least conception. Yet such realms would still be no more than shadows, projections, the mere frontiers of Reality.

Your reading of the great mystics should have shown, however, that the veil hiding inexpressible mysteries is not absolutely impenetrable.

Those who have sought truth with love and reverence combined with wisdom have attained to a greater realization of some aspects of the Godhead—the All-in-All-United—than any other spiritual adventurers.

But none of them have ever truly succeeded in speaking of what they knew beyond stumbling words, symbols and analogies which, as they themselves freely admitted, revealed virtually nothing of the Reality they had glimpsed still "within a glass darkly".

But even such faint glimmerings were only attained by years, probably whole lives, devoted to an ardent search and the kind of spiritual practices and disciplines of which I have given you the merest outline. Yet the knowledge that such seekers should have attained to these heights of vision can inspire you with courage and hope. The fact that, in this life, you feel such an ardent desire for understanding shows that your own search has not been only initiated in this present incarnation.

In our modern age even such faint insights into the nature of ultimate Reality are rare because man is currently engaged in developing his mental faculties as never before. Consequently the more evolved and sensitive are unduly exposed to the pressures of an intensely extrovert and materialistic phase of evolution. It will pass. It is already passing. But you must remember that these great cycles of development take years to come to their peak and even longer to decline.

Do not mistake what I have just said to mean that I am denying the vital importance of the full development of the mental faculties. All new ideas and theories, even religious and spiritual ones, must pass through the filter of the alert and critical mind in order that wishful thinking, pure fantasy and prejudice be eliminated by the exercise of integrity and discrimination; but too much should not be expected of them. The attitude I advocate is that of the true scientist tempered by some attributes of the mystical intuitive approach. Indeed many scientists are beginning to recognize that they are reaching the limits of the material world and stand on the frontiers of another.

It is indeed a razor-edged path that the aspirant to wisdom has to tread; but the more acutely he is aware of this the more safely will he advance.

So do not let yourself be over-concerned by your present limitations or even about the actual degree of your progress. This indicates a too great concentration on the personality. The answer is: Walk on and work from the highest level you can reach in every situation which confronts you and you will do well.

It is foolish for anyone to expect to reach the top of the mountain in one bound. It would serve you nothing if you could, for the air would be too rarified for you to breathe. Indeed we are told that even the flower of humanity, those now out of incarnation as well as other beings on even higher reaches of the spiritual heights, still remain ignorant of inconceivably vast reaches of the nature of the One Life which on earth reveals itself most perfectly through the expressions and powers of love.

Nor is there any need for you to feel that the areas of understanding which still evade you are essential to your progress. At these early stages too much concentration on the deeper mysteries can even prevent it. So can too much concentration on esoteric knowledge, for this does not necessarily give a man wisdom or love. You are here to deal with the problems of your present stage of evolution wisely and efficiently with as much spiritual help from your Soul as you are capable of invoking. Metaphysic is *not* a substitute for living although its insights can act as inspiration and as guides.

It is even possible to get lost in its labyrinths and so neglect natural duty on the physical plane. This is a mistake made by far too many immature people who try to run before they can walk, much less fly, and so fall into many pits of dogma, half-truths and false ideas about their own spiritual status which impede rather than aid them in living the good life.

It suffices at present that you have become far more aware than ever before of the specific weaknesses and blocks which hitherto have prevented your progress towards a more balanced and therefore more health-giving outlook on life and that you now realize to an increasing degree that you are ready to make the attempt to take a further step away from your old false attitudes of separateness towards greater and wider realizations.

Yet I would impress upon you once again that as you follow this path upon which you have now set your feet, occasional glimpses of higher levels of consciousness, moments of sudden vision, clearer realization of the interpenetration of the material world by the divine effulgence, will come to you. But never try deliberately to force entry through these gates of perception. Such experiences come at first always as a gift. They may do so in meditation, through reading, or by the sudden near-miraculous transformation of some quite ordinary object, when it seems as if Life Itself leaps out to greet you in order to prove to you that, veritably, It dwells in all things. Nature and music will probably be, for you, the best media of revelation, since it is their language which speaks most clearly to your heart. But realize too that such glimpses are always transmitted to the personality from the higher Self in which this quality of perception resides. They are an earnest of what permanent en-Soulment of the personality holds for all.

What is of vital importance is that this search for Reality must always be powered by devotion to the highest ideals. It must also be carried on with patience and a determination which never fails in the face of defeat or disaster or, what is perhaps hardest to bear, the discovery that some of your deductions and theories have been founded upon falsely interpreted premises.

But this is less likely to happen if you always keep in mind that it is the "sight" of the Soul which is the power to be invoked when you seek for truth at any level. For its special quality is its ability to participate in what might be called the "pool" of wisdom available to all who can attain to the plane upon which it can be tapped.

Here is yet another reason why regular meditation is so vitally important; this tends to attune you to that plane by concentration upon whatever concept or hypothesis you are seeking to elucidate.

And as you succeed in perfecting this inner technique so you will become the recipient of the inflow of many forces from other and higher levels.

The way to touch these heights may be through the passionate search for and worship of truth—that of the scientist; or of the musician, artist, poet, all who are affiliated closely with the realms of those creative Beings who have been called the great Imaginals. Or it may be the way of yoga, of those who train themselves through understanding of the inner laws governing body and mind. But perhaps it is most easily attained by the mystics and all who see God in every created thing but most of all love their fellow men.

By whatever road they come, each eventually reaches the sacred mountain. Possibly during the long journey through time, man travels upon every one of these roads, thus perfecting himself in all aspects of his being.

But in order to reach the highest peak of perfection possible to man in the flesh and to catch glimpses of supernal beauty, truth and glory, self-discipline and dedication are absolutely essential. To the undisciplined and unbalanced personality the pressures released by too much intensive concentration on the higher levels can be so great that he risks being overwhelmed by the forces emanating from them, unless he has prepared himself wisely in many lives to be able to meet them from his own spiritual centre. If he has not done this he may not be able to sustain the vision of the gods which may even destroy him just as, in the legend, the sight of the glorious countenance of Zeus destroyed Semele.

I have emphasized this danger more than once during these talks, but it is very easily forgotten. There are no short cuts in this adventure into the higher regions of the unknown. Any form of over-stimulation is dangerous here, so a high degree of balance is essential.

Drugs or psychic practices can take a man down into the fantasies of his own subconscious or deeper still into the region of the dark chimeras created by the human race in its long journey towards the light. I repeat: *There are no short cuts,* so never let yourself be carried away by excess of zeal.

The true healing you seek demands the acquisition of balance and integration; so how could it be anything but slow since it entails a gradual preparation of the body, emotions and the mind in order to change all their ancient habits and rhythms? What I have given you in these preliminary instructions should be enough for this life, probably even for the next; but that depends upon yourself. You realize now how much has to be undone, and how much repaired and strengthened.

What I have endeavoured to achieve is only to set your

feet upon the true way of preparation for a continuous advance, along the road to perfect and permanent health.

But I would impress upon you yet again that every effort you make to heal yourself as I have taught you to do must have an effect. You may become conscious of this even in this present life. That is my hope.

You have indeed progressed far already upon what has been called the path to the Path. Soon, if you persist in your efforts the next step will confront you, for you possess the inner determination, the faith, courage and above all the aspiration which are absolutely essential in such a quest.

Had not these potentialities already existed in your present personality it would not have been possible for me to have made this close contact with you nor for you to have made as much progress in this short time as you have done.

Meditate upon this until we meet again.

XVI

This is the last treatment that I can give you, therefore it would be as well if I recalled to your memory the most important aspects of my attempt to show you how you can achieve healing in the true meaning of that word.

You understand now the reasons why any cure, to be genuine and lasting, must be so deep and radical that no part of the total personality can be excluded, and that to achieve this the first step is to recognize the need to be able to invoke a greater power than your own, that of your Soul.

In order to do this you must learn to align yourself with it by using the methods and techniques we have been studying together and by acquiring the ability to recognize its vibration and obey the impulses which, as the bridge between these two aspects of yourself becomes stronger, will enable its power and wisdom to flow ever more freely and constructively into every activity of your existence at every level.

The genuine efforts you have made while I have been in touch with you should have proved to you that this can be done. It may have even seemed at rare moments comparatively easy; but I must warn you that the fact that you have been able occasionally to reach up to these higher levels of your consciousness is mainly due to your having been put in unusually close contact with your Soul through what I can only call an artificial stimulus.

But this cannot last unless, by adopting from now on an entirely new orientation to every aspect of life, you yourself provide the conditions in which it can take place. This means, as you know, clearing the channels by your own efforts at the personality level so that the light may be enabled to stream through and so achieve a greater unity throughout your whole being.

I have already warned you many times that at such an early stage you must not expect immediate results. While the process of reorientation and rebuilding is taking place there will be inevitable setbacks and even periods of intense darkness—termed "dryness" by the great mystics—which will seem even harder to bear in contrast to these recent experiences.

When this happens remember that such phases of darkness, like pains in the body, can be of real value so long as you understand their cause and do not allow yourself to be too disheartened. For just as pain makes you aware that something is wrong and warns you to look for its cause and cure, so these phases of special difficulty can be reminders, messages, stimulants which could induce you to make special efforts to bestir yourself and invoke with greater determination these powers which will always respond to a genuine call for renewed help and strength.

By forcing you thus to concentrate upon your "life-line" instead of fixing attention upon your troubles at lower levels, you will be enabled to achieve increased contact with your Soul.

You have come, at last, to accept the fact that man *is* perfectable. This is one of the vital steps in his journey in search of wholeness of being.

But you must also keep in mind that in order to attain this "pearl of great price" it is necessary at some time or another to be prepared to relinquish many lesser prizes and to make a genuine attempt to follow the councils of those more spiritually advanced than yourself who, all down the ages, have dedicated their lives in the attempt to enlighten mankind.

But here I would stress that knowledge of their teachings is not enough; that even the wisdom of the Scriptures is not enough, nor is the example of the Great Ones. These are all invaluable guides since they reveal aspects of the one true and *universal* Way to liberation from sickness, sorrow and despair.

But these teachings can even become hindrances and dangers if the seeker attaches himself *emotionally* and fanatically to any one, excluding all others. What is essential is that, having found the specific approach which best suits his temperament and outlook, he should *live it out* applying it down to the smallest details of life, however apparently insignificant. For unless the teaching can be experienced in action and proved to work, he cannot know that his choice is the correct one. This, after all, is the only valid test of any experiment.

Once the specific path has been chosen and the methods it advocates been proved then the success of the journey depends entirely upon putting the precepts into practice with patience, endurance, determination and *faith*. Faith (by which I do not mean blind faith) is essential because, however many times you fail, however harsh the difficulties you are called upon to face and however long it takes before any real advance can be recognized, you must continue to hold the conviction that you, like all other human beings, *are* perfectable and that the goal *can* be attained.

Remind yourself, when doubts arise, that the wisdom of the ages insists that man is a god in embryo and his destiny is to become one in full consciousness.

So walk on courageously through the dark valley with your eyes fixed on the beckoning light ahead, armed with all you have now acquired in understanding and reassurance.

For you have at last experienced, if only for a flash of a second, not theoretically but as a living truth, what the result of a linking up with your Soul can achieve. Such knowledge can never be wholly lost or forgotten although it can, of course, be temporarily overlaid by the pressures of the world and sink into oblivion.

Do not let this happen again. For it did happen to you once in your past. Then you knew these truths; you even tried to act in accordance with them. But you forgot. The mists of self-will, ambition, hate swept in and obliterated all memory of the shining heights and the path to their attainment. But the knowledge lay hidden, as a treasure is hidden by a fall of rock, until eventually a strong impetus had to be applied by the Soul so that the need for help became great enough to revive faint memories of what had once been known. Hence your present difficult life.

A change in consciousness had become sufficiently far advanced in your last life to cause faint memories and vague aspirations to be astir in you since early childhood. But it was also because a special effort at recall had been made in an earlier life that help could be given now and this specific method of instruction through an intermediary has been permitted.

There is an old saying that when a pupil is ready a master appears.

Such a "master" may take many forms—a sudden flash of enlightenment, a passage read in a book, a friend pointing the way. But because *like alone can apprehend like* it is idle, as so many do, to run around seeking a "guru". More often than not if one should present himself he is no more than the reflection of the aspirant's secret vanity or pride. In any case it is not the personality which directs him who is ready to receive truth and instruction to the right quarters, it is the Soul.

You have now been shown how to begin the process of permanent healing yourself. Help will be given you so that you may remain in this body for just as long as Karma permits and your Soul feels it desirable. In fact until you have come to the end of what it is possible for you to achieve in your present personality.

In the meantime it will be to members of the medical faculty and any other healers on the physical plane in whom you can have confidence that you will be directed. They will keep you in sufficiently good health to enable you to continue your work here as long as necessary.

One thing I would impress upon you. Do not imagine that you must be in any way unique for having had an experience that I must call, for want of a better word, artificial precipitation of help and training; nor fall into the delusion that you have been especially favoured. There are no favours in the realms in which the Soul operates. No one ever gets less or more than they have earned in some phase of their long journey through time or need in their present phase of development.

In any case such a special effort at communication as this is never made for the personality alone to whom it comes. The objective is far wider. An opportunity presents itself to those with vision and is taken; the appropriate mechanism is at hand and is used. When the need to defeat the forces of materialism is as great as it is today every weapon, however imperfect in itself, must be used.

I have pointed out already that humanity is now at the very nadir of materialism and consequently is passing through a period of acute crisis, one of the most acute ever experienced. This could mean a turning-point in evolution if a greater proportion of mankind could be roused from its spiritual apathy and enabled to rise to the opportunities for enlightenment which such a crisis affords.

But everything depends upon whether sufficient spiritual power can be invoked by all those with vision in order to counteract the dark forces of greed, self-interest, violence and sheer blindness which could otherwise precipitate the world into perhaps the most terrible disaster humanity has ever experienced.

In view of this danger every gleam of spiritual understanding, every aspect of goodwill, every advance towards deeper and more fruitful relationships between nations and individuals, everything, in short, that makes in any way for unification and harmony, is being stimulated and encouraged whenever it can be discerned by those who watch over and seek to guide humanity.

Consequently everyone who is capable of being aroused from absorption in self is being given special help and encouragement to join in what is truly a work of redemption.

This is the reason why I have stressed constantly in these talks the necessity for you to recognize and to accept your personal responsibility as a cell in the body of mankind and to work at making it a healthy cell radiating light and life.

Your thank-offering for all you have received must now be to work unceasingly to fit yourself to play an increasing part in this great spiritual effort at salvage.

This you have the capacity to do in your own specialized field through which you can spread the knowledge of true healing and the teachings you have been given. Thus you can also help to swell the streams of love and power which are being poured down upon the planet at this time in the attempt to strengthen all those men of good-will who are working here in their many ways to co-operate, whether they are consciously aware of it or not, with all others at higher levels who are fighting on the side of humanity.

And when it seems to you to be a hopeless task and you despair—as you often will—at your own helplessness and impotence; when the dark clouds of humanity's suffering threaten to overwhelm you, remember that in allying yourself with the forces of light you are also working not only for greater happiness and peace in your own life now, but for the next life also. You are not only seeking to perfect that tiny spark which you are, in order that it may send its beam into the dark, confused and chaotic world about you, but also that it may become a clear and shining flame in the future.

Recall again that saying of Jesus which I have quoted to you so often: *To him that hath shall be given.* As you strive to use to the full the knowledge you have invoked to help you on your way with increasing determination, wisdom and courage—for courage too will often be needed—you will be developing the capacity to receive more from the endless store in the universal treasure house of the spirit.

So now I, the teacher you called to yourself by your inner readiness to accept and to apply this universal remedy for all forms of sickness, must leave you.

But in truth you will never be left without a teacher unless you cut yourself off from that interior Voice of which every teacher and spiritual healer is a representative. For they are all symbols in their degrees, of aspects of those great redemptive Powers which have endeavoured from the beginning of man's sojourn in the density of matter to release him from its thrall of ignorance. Their voices speak through each individual Soul to the personality which has learned to be attentive; for truly, in a sense, these are all faint echoes of one Voice—that of the Divine Physician—the Christ spirit.

My whole endeavour in these talks has been to put you in touch with your own particular aspect of that universal Voice. It is for you, from now on, to keep the lines of communication open.

Your Soul, your own teacher who is indeed "closer than breathing, nearer than hands or feet", will never leave you, even when you may ignore him. How could he? He is your essential self.

So, retire as often as you can into the silence in order to train the inner ear to distinguish this voice among the clamorous voices within and outside you. Learn to wire-in to this wavelength so that in times of need you will always be enabled easily to establish contact with a part of yourself which is wiser than the personality in which you have been for long ages so deeply entombed.

But when you listen, remember my earlier warning. For a long time to come you must be on your guard against hearing what those "little selves" within you want you to hear. Use your intelligence, practical common sense as well as your intuition. They will all be needed to prevent wishes, fears and hopes blurring the message.

Eventually, if you persevere, the voice which has been relayed to you during this short period in the tones and language of the physical plane will be replaced by that Voice which will never leave you.

At times when you feel yourself totally cut off, unable to wire-in, possibly not even wishing to do so owing to the heaviness of material conditions, try to recall deliberately all you have been told; make an effort to stand aside from the concerns of the personality and search for the cause of this short-circuit, for you may be sure of one thing—it will certainly arise from some level of your own being. So never put the blame upon outer conditions or other people. Only the ignorant do so.

I would leave you with this final reassurance. If you persist despite every setback in trying to put into effect the various techniques I have suggested to you, you will most surely at last be enabled to tune-in at will to the wavelength of your Soul. Later you may even, through increasing contact with it, reach to higher levels still. For, as I have insisted so often, just as you, the personality, strain upward to that plane upon which your Soul functions, so It seeks ever higher sources of wisdom and spiritual insight which are still far beyond Its own reach.

Finally I would remind you yet again that the greatest power of renewal and of healing is love—love in its many aspects, for love is the revelation to man of divine

Imminence. Seek then to express it in all you do and let your thoughts be always attuned to it. Thus one day your whole life will become an expression on earth of this divine energy and an instrument for its use.

So, child of earth and heaven, let love henceforth be your guide at all times through the mazes of life in the form, that love which beautifies and enhances every manifestation of existence. Practice compassion for every creature, but above all for your fellow men and women, so many of whom live still in darkness, fear and hate. Enter into their sorrows and pains by imagination, insight and above all by intuitive identification.

Do not forget that love always expresses itself through giving; not necessarily of material things, which is relatively easy and often serves as an excuse for failing to give time, thought, understanding and indeed the very self. It is by developing this quality of the giving of your Whole Self to the utmost that you will be freed from the burden of your separate selfhood, of that obsession with its limitations which has held you prisoner for so long.

And at all times endeavour also to cultivate an attitude of joyousness, the radiation of light; for this is the reflection of that creative energy which heals and renews, Light is Life.

Never forget that the greater becomes your own ability to love, the nearer you will come to understanding something of the true nature of Divinity.

The more perfectly you can, in your own sphere, be it never so limited, embody the outgoing energy of love, the more fully will this greater love illuminate your whole being and disclose to you its secrets.

And in the degree to which you can learn to practice love, in the same degree will you gain, not only joy and serenity despite all the vicissitudes of life, but the capacity to become yourself a source of peace and healing.

And when you succeed—as one day, sooner or late,

you surely will—in identifying your entire consciousness with the very Source of love, all separative desires will vanish, all words be superfluous.

You will be whole, for you will become the flame within the Flame and your goal will be attained.

Peace be with you.

May love flow in and through and around you in an ever-increasing tide of glory.

May the Light within unite with the Light without; may they fuse, may they blend, may they blaze forth.

May the design be accomplished and your destiny fulfilled.

APPENDIX

Hold fast to the thought of the eternal spirit of love through all your pain;

Feel it enfolding you, filling you, giving you life;

In the darkest moments invoke it, that it may flow into your heart;

By holding this thought ever present in your mind courage will be born, strength generated, fear banished.

You will know with absolute certainty that no aspiration towards a state of love and harmony can beget aught but these same powers in your being.

Use love as a spear to pierce the darkness. It will rend it asunder and you will at last know Reality in place of illusion;

Light will be released from where it eternally dwells hidden within you; it will blaze forth; it will envelop you gloriously.

* * *

Seek to understand the nature of unity;

Seek to understand the spiritual significance of conflict.

Without conflict there could be no development, no progress;

How could light be comprehended without darkness?

You who are only a temporary dweller in a body, despise nothing, ignore nothing, fear nothing.

Each part must speak in the language appropriate to it and all these languages must be understood in order that the parts can be directed aright.

Love is the key-language to which they all respond. Love is the solvent of all conflicts.

Through love alone can the little lives of the body learn
   to become a united and harmonious whole.
Let them obey their Master—the Soul.
So ignore nothing—fear nothing—hate nothing.
Accept what is needful, even pain, even frustration.
See them as part of a total work of perfection.
Use them creatively and they will lead you to your goal.

* * *

I would have you realize that after death all the subtle
atoms which have been held together by the magnetic
attraction of the Soul are dispersed, entering into other
forms. See to it, therefore, that they be so impregnated
by the powers of the Good, the True and the Beautiful
during the time they are under your influence that wher-
ever they are dispersed they carry into their new forms no
germs of conflict, sorrow and fear engendered by your
thoughts and acts, but are carriers of light, joy and peace.

Remember that you are veritably responsible for all that
has been yours while on earth and for the future of your
substance in its reincarnation in form.

May you become a benefactor of earth-life even when
you have departed from it!

* * *

Relax and feel yourself absorbing the light of healing
   and regeneration, that power which, vibrating through
   your bodies, unites you to the rhythm of the universe.
Let all your thoughts seek to express the will of the
   Divine working through form to uplift, to enlighten, to
   bring realization.
Breathe in harmony;
Breathe out harmony.
Let harmony be expressed by every little life within you.

Respond throughout your being to the note of love and
joy.
In all you do sound forth the note of love which is the
note of the spirit.
Realize the livingness of that Light within you.
Let it blaze forth;
Let it purify and glorify all about you.
Let it begin the work of constructing for Itself a new,
harmonious, healthy vehicle of expression.
Hold fast to the knowledge that there is in essence nothing
but the Good; only your understanding is dark as yet
and perceives it not.

*   *   *

Seek to manifest love with ever-increasing perfection
and love will manifest in you and in all about you so
powerfully that fear will be cast out. No longer will you
flee from experience, even from sorrow or sickness,
rather will you receive and embrace them. In such an
act of pure submission to the greater will of the divine,
sorrow, sickness, doubt and fear will be transmuted,
burned up in the fire of love.

*   *   *

Oh, child who feel yourself to be a separate part of That
which is Unity;
Unite yourself to It through love.
Let all that is within manifest its rhythm, respond to the
universal beat of the divine heart;
Take part in the dance of creation.
Launch yourself without fear upon the mighty ocean of
love which flows endlessly throughout the cosmos;
Although to your eyes in the trough of its waves there is
darkest shadow, remember their movement is ever

forward and upward and if you can abandon yourself to it without fear, without struggle and shrinking, you must inevitably be borne along to the further shore on their glittering crests.

Those who have learned the secrets of the wise do not sink into this seeming darkness.

You shall be one of these; as a flight of a bird winging its way from crest to crest, riding joyously in the sunlight; this shall be your life.

Remember this Ocean combines all Elements.

The earth is its bed, where darkness lingers for those who cannot yet rise towards the light. Herein are all forms conceived.

Here is the womb where the germ sleeps before its awakening.

This is the plane of matter which you must learn to use, but which must not be allowed to hold you down. This also is love.

The waters of emotion are the mighty waves. Control therefore emotion, be no longer submerged by it. Used aright it will lift you up into the air—for it also is love.

Air is the mind; the medium through which the consuming fire of the sun is tempered to your weakness, transmuted and modified for your use—for here also is love.

And the Fire of the Sun is the Flame of selfless devotion, the burning ecstasy of love in its fulness.

Rise therefore through all elements that you may perfectly express in every aspect the glory of your Lord.

* * *

Live in peace.

Think peace.

Let there be harmony in every thought and every act, in every wish and desire and you will so transform your life and the atmosphere about you that an increasing measure of fulfilment will be possible.

Accept and seek to understand all that affects your life;
Everything destructive will then depart; everything
   harmful be transmuted.
Use every experience for good—and it will bring you
   good.

Invocation to the Soul

Sound forth the note that banishes the illusion of
   separateness, fear, unreason and unrest!
Let a beam of your Light shine through this your vehicle
   of manifestation in matter!
Control it! Guide it! Perfect it!
Help it to become a true reflection on earth of your
   spiritual being!
Make it fit to serve you, yours to use, yours to illuminate
   with knowledge, wisdom and love!

QUEST BOOKS

are published by The Theosophical
Society in America, a branch of
a world organization dedicated to the
promotion of brotherhood and the
encouragement of the study of religion,
philosophy, and science, to the end
that man may better understand
himself and his place in the universe.
The Society stands for complete
freedom of individual search and belief.
Quest Books are offered as a
contribution to man's search for truth.